THE Gospel OF Happiness

ALSO BY CHRISTOPHER KACZOR

The Seven Big Myths about the Catholic Church

How to Stay Catholic in College

The Seven Big Myths about Marriage

Life Issues, Medical Choices

O Rare Ralph McInerny: Stories and Reflections on a Legendary Notre Dame Professor

Thomas Aquinas on Faith, Hope, and Love

Thomas Aquinas on the Cardinal Virtues

THE Gospel OF Happiness

Rediscover Your Faith Through Spiritual Practice and Positive Psychology

CHRISTOPHER KACZOR

IMAGE
New York

Published in the United States by Image, an imprint of the Crown Publishing Group, a division of Penguin Random House LLC, New York.
www.crownpublishing.com

IMAGE is a registered trademark and the "I" colophon is a trademark of Penguin Random House LLC.

Grateful acknowledgment is made to Avery, an imprint of Penguin Publishing Group for permission to reprint scattered excerpts from *The Willpower Instinct: How Self-Control Works, Why It Matters, and What You Can Do to Get More of It* by Kelly McGonigal, copyright © 2012 by Kelly McGonigal, PhD. Used by permission of Avery, an imprint of Penguin Publishing Group, a division of Penguin Random House LLC.

Library of Congress Cataloging-in-Publication Data is available upon request.

ISBN 978-0-8041-4100-0
eBook ISBN 978-0-8041-4101-7

Printed in the United States of America

Jacket design by FORT

10 9 8 7 6 5 4 3 2 1

First Edition

For Kevin, *amicus amico*

Jesus prayed, saying: "Holy Father, . . . I speak this in the world so that they may share my joy completely."

John 17:1, 13

All people seek happiness. This is without exception. Whatever different means they employ, they all tend to this end. The cause of some going to war, and of others avoiding it, is the same desire in both, attended with different views. The will never takes the least step but to this object. This is the motive of every action of every person, even of those who hang themselves.

Blaise Pascal, *Pensées,* 425

| CONTENTS |

| ACKNOWLEDGMENTS |

I am deeply indebted to numerous people who helped this project immeasurably. I'd like to mention in particular Gregg Ten Elshof, Thomas Crisp, and Steve Porter, the directors of Biola University's Center for Christian Thought. This publication benefited from a research fellowship at Biola University's Center for Christian Thought, which was made possible through the support of a grant from the John Templeton Foundation. The opinions expressed in this publication are those of the author and do not necessarily reflect the views of the John Templeton Foundation or Biola's Center for Christian Thought. I am also indebted to Todd W. Hall, Peter C. Hill, Eric L. Johnson, Jonathan Lunde, Alan G. Padgett, Judy Ten Elshof, Dan Crowley, Betsy A. Barber, John H. Coe, C. Stephen Evans, David A. Horner, Kelly M. Kapic, Greg Peters, William Struthers, James Wilhoit, Ken Tang-Quan, and Todd Pickett, who participated in our weekly roundtable meetings.

I'd also especially like to thank Dave Strobolakos, Mariele Courtis, and Nicole Garcia for helping me as research assistants on this and other projects. I am also deeply grateful to Aaron Kheriaty, Miles Kessler, David R. Oakley, Esq., Heidi Giebel, and Kaye Cook for reading and commenting on the manuscript. My wife, Jennifer, kindly provided a first draft of several paragraphs. I am especially indebted to Gary Jansen, the editor at Image Books at Penguin Random House. He nourished this project from its initial stages to its completion by his kindness, support, and critical eye for improvement.

Finally, I would like to acknowledge that the completion of this project took place during my appointment as William E. Simon Visiting Fellow in Religion and Public Life in the James Madison Program at Princeton University. I am grateful to Robert P. George, director of the James Madison Program, and Brad Wilson, the executive director, for being such wonderful hosts.

Christopher Kaczor
Princeton University

| INTRODUCTION |

What is real happiness? How can I experience it? How can I live it? Every thoughtful person asks such questions. Thoughtful Christians add a few more questions, such as: How can I enhance Christian living? Is there any proof that Christian practices enhance happiness? Does Christianity provide happiness in a way that other paths, like psychology, cannot?

These questions are worth exploring, but I never expected to write a book like this looking at happiness from a theological and psychological perspective. My only personal experience in psychological counseling had not been positive. As a graduate student studying philosophy and theology at the University of Notre Dame, I was under tremendous academic and financial pressure. I wanted to be a philosophy professor, but I wasn't sure if I had what it took to make it. My wife and I were struggling to support our young family of three children on my graduate stipend of $10,000 a year. Financial pressure, family struggles, and the intensity of my academic work took a toll. A friend suggested I seek psychological counseling, so

I did. After the second session, the psychologist said to me, "You know, Chris, there are two kinds of people for whom psychological counseling is completely worthless. One group is hard-core drug addicts. The other group is philosophers." Needless to say, there was no third session.

So, although my initial experience with a psychologist had not proved helpful, in reading about the philosophy and theology of happiness, my scholarly work on the subject of happiness eventually led me to something called "positive psychology," which opened my eyes anew.

When Martin Seligman of the University of Pennsylvania was elected president of the American Psychological Association in 1998, he chose "positive psychology" as his theme, launching a new movement within the field. Traditionally, psychology has focused on people's problems such as depression, anxiety, and bipolar disorder. Seligman challenged psychologists to find empirical answers for new questions, such as: What makes people happier? How can people become more resilient? What are people's signature strengths?

Seligman's recasting of psychology opened up a flourishing new field that focused on optimism rather than helplessness, signature strengths rather than pathology, and growth in happiness rather than depression. Tal Ben-Shahar, author of *Happier: Learn the Secrets to Daily Joy and Lasting Fulfillment*, began teaching about positive psychology, and his class became Harvard's most popular undergraduate course. The University of Pennsylvania and Claremont Graduate University now offer advanced degrees in positive psychology. This new field also generated bestselling books such as *The How of Happiness: A Scientific Approach to Getting the Life You Want*, by

Sonja Lyubomirsky, professor of psychology at the University of California, Riverside. Unlike Norman Vincent Peale and his idea of the power of positive thinking, researchers in positive psychology stress that their approach is empirical and scientific. Like new medications, the various strategies for increasing happiness are tested via double-blind, replicated studies that make use of control groups.

What I learned from positive psychology was astonishing. First, although some people believe that faith and psychology contradict each other, researchers in positive psychology found that traditional Christian practices such as giving thanks, forgiving others, and serving your neighbor promoted human happiness and well-being. I learned that I did not need to choose between Christian faith and positive psychology, any more than I had to choose between Christian faith and modern medicine. Christian believers can embrace the findings of positive psychology, even if its source is secular science. As St. Augustine wrote in *On Christian Doctrine,* "Let every good and true Christian understand that wherever truth may be found, it belongs to his Master."[1] St. Thomas Aquinas had the same insight: "Every truth, no matter who utters it, comes from the Holy Spirit."[2] Indeed, positive psychology vindicates the wisdom of Christian practices. Some philosophers, like Friedrich Nietzsche, claim that Christian practices undermine a flourishing human life. But positive psychology provides empirical evidence that Christian practices, such as forgiveness, service, and love of neighbor, enhance human well-being.

Second, I discovered that certain contemporary findings in psychology can help Christians to better live the message of Jesus. The Second Vatican Council envisioned such uses of science: "In pastoral care, sufficient use must be made, not only of theological principles, but also of the findings of the secular sciences, especially of psychology and sociology, so that the faithful may be brought to a more adequate and mature life of faith" (*Gaudium et Spes* 62). In this book, I hope to put into practice this teaching of the Second Vatican Council by showing how positive psychology can enhance Christian living.

I had always thought that psychology was an *alternative* to religion. In college, I had read Sigmund Freud's attack on Christian belief. Freud, the founder of twentieth-century psychology, taught that religion was an illusion, and he wrote that he hoped "that in the future science will go beyond religion, and reason will replace faith in God."[3] After I'd read Freud's view of religion, the idea that psychology and faith are diametrically opposed became cemented in the back of my mind. But Freud's views—about both religion and psychology—have been challenged in a variety of ways, in part by findings based on empirical evidence.[4] Contemporary psychology does make use of some Freudian insights, but psychologists do not need to adopt his atheism and hostility to religion. Practicing positive psychology certainly does not necessitate atheism. Indeed, I found that positive psychology is connected in surprising ways with the practice of faith.

Positive psychology provides an independent verification of the happiness-boosting power of many traditional Christian practices. St. Thomas Aquinas saw in Aristotelian philosophy a powerful way to show—using reason alone—that the many truths of the Christian faith were also reasonable. Using philosophy, he was able to point to a God who was one, all-powerful, all-knowing, and all-good. In a similar way, positive psychology provides a powerful justification—using reason alone—for practicing Christian virtues, such as forgiveness, humility, gratitude, and love for others.

The current Christian's situation with respect to psychology is somewhat analogous to thirteenth-century Christians' engagement with Aristotle. When Aristotle was rediscovered in that era, some Christians feared and condemned the errors of his thinking. But this rediscovery led other Christians, in particular St. Albert the Great and St. Thomas Aquinas, to investigate this philosophy more deeply, and out of this investigation, these saints forged a new and powerful synthesis of Greek philosophy and Christian revelation. Although some manifestations and approaches in psychology are clearly incompatible and vitiate Christian faith, positive psychology offers both surprising confirmations of Christian practice and helpful aids for Christian living. Just as Aristotle's natural theology bolstered Christian theology, today positive psychology provides an empirical justification and aid for Christian practice, a kind of natural moral theology.

It might seem as if seeking after flourishing and happiness runs counter to the Christian message: To be a Christian is about doing one's duty, not seeking happiness. Being a practicing Christian is about loving your neighbor altruistically and serving God sacrificially; it's not about getting personal satisfaction.

Certainly, the Christian life involves loving neighbor and loving God rather than selfishly seeking personal satisfaction at other people's expense. But part of the Christian message is that authentic happiness is to be found not in selfishness, but in self-giving. The Gospel message is not an alternative to but a way to freedom, meaning, and happiness. As Pope Francis notes, "The joy of the gospel fills the hearts and lives of all who encounter Jesus. Those who accept his offer of salvation are set free from sin, sorrow, inner emptiness and loneliness. With Christ joy is constantly born anew."[5] The Christian way in its fullness, even in its sacrifices for love, is a path to happiness, fulfillment, and joy, not an alternative to happiness, fulfillment, and joy.

In this book, I highlight the many ways in which positive psychology and Christian practice overlap. I point out empirical findings in positive psychology that point to the wisdom of many Christian practices and teachings. I also provide practical suggestions on how to become happier in everyday life and how to deepen Christian practice based on contemporary psychological insights. All of this points us toward deeper fulfillment in this life, and in the life to come. This is why I've titled this book *The Gospel of Happiness*—because this is good news, very good news indeed.

THE Gospel OF Happiness

| ONE |

The Ways to Happiness

In his book *Flourish: A Visionary New Understanding of Happiness and Well-Being,* Martin Seligman proposes that happiness, which he also calls "flourishing" and "well-being," involves five elements: positive emotion, engagement, relationships, meaning, and achievement (PERMA).[1] This sounds about right to me. The best times of my life—the birth of my eldest child, Elizabeth, minutes after I thought she was dying; walking up with my children clad either in white dress or white tie as they received their First Holy Communion; seeing the Golden Dome of the University of Notre Dame for the first time—involved some mix of positive emotion, engagement, relationships, meaning, and achievement. Critics of Christianity sometimes believe that faith promises heavenly happiness as a substitute and replacement for happiness on earth. Fast on bread and water now, feast on steak and lobster in the life to come. In fact, Christian belief and practice help people become happier not just in heaven but also on earth. In exploring positive psychology, I discovered anew that grace, as it were, fulfills nature.

The Way of Positive Emotion

The first way to human flourishing is *positive emotions* such as joy, delight, warmth, euphoria, and gladness. Researchers measure positive emotion or subjective well-being through asking people questions such as "How happy are you right now?" or "How satisfied are you with your life?"[2]

Imagine a beeper goes off right now. How would you rate your level of happiness? If the beeper went off during the course of a typical day—as you sipped your morning coffee, as the traffic slowed down because of a minor collision, or during a walk at dusk through pine trees in the park—you'd likely report a variety of positive and negative emotions. After decades of collecting such data, scientists have discovered some clear trends about positive emotion.

Scientists discovered that those who practice a religious faith report less depression and more positive emotion. In his book *The Pursuit of Happiness,* the psychologist David Myers notes, "Survey after survey across North America and Europe reveals that religious people more often than nonreligious people report being happy and satisfied with life."[3] People who strongly believe in God are more than twice as likely to report being happy as those who do not believe in God. When researchers examined religious practices, such as attending church, they found a link between worship and reported happiness. Eighty-six percent of people who attend church services weekly report being "satisfied" or "very satisfied" with life.[4] Notice that these trends are about those who practice religious faith, not merely have religious faith. The man who professes belief in God but who lives as if God does not exist, skipping church to watch the Broncos play the Seahawks, is unlikely to experience the positive effects reported by the researchers.

Researchers also found that people who practice a religious faith are less likely to suffer from intense negative feelings such as depression. The psychiatrist Aaron Kheriaty points out:

> Studies among adults consistently reveal lower rates of depression among individuals who are more religiously observant. The vast majority of these studies looked at Christian patients. . . . More than a hundred research studies have examined the relationship between religion and depression. Two-thirds of these found fewer depressive symptoms in those who were more religious. Only 5 percent of these studies found that being more religious was associated with more depression. Out of twenty-two long-term studies, fifteen found that greater religious practice (prayer, church attendance, Scripture reading) predicted milder symptoms and more rapid recovery.[5]

Religious practice alleviates depressive symptoms and enhances positive feeling and satisfaction with life.

Some Christians might be tempted to think that all that really matters, at least morally speaking, are your actions, especially doing your duty, not whether or not you are experiencing positive emotions. Indeed, it might seem that being concerned about one's emotions is a selfish preoccupation that conflicts with the demands of Christian duty, which is understood as cultivating an altruistic regard for others. Phyllis Zagano and C. Kevin Gillespie, SJ, express this concern: "Positive Psychology can appear as a self-seeking and self-serving process aimed simply at obtaining individual and interpersonal happiness."[6] The volunteer ladling onion soup to the homeless teen is the Christian saint, not the person selfishly seeking to feel good.

Certainly, Christians are called to love God and neighbor regardless of how they might be feeling at the moment. It would indeed be a grave mistake to think that the ultimate goal of life was simply to experience positive emotions. Although what we do is vitally important regardless of how we are feeling, it is unhelpful to moral growth to belittle the importance of emotions and feelings that can promote or hinder leading a morally good life. When we feel upset, depressed, sad, and angry, we can still do the right thing, but doing the right thing while experiencing negative emotions becomes immensely more difficult. Especially when experiencing intense depression, anxiety, sadness, or grief, people tend to focus on themselves and are strongly prompted to seek relief from their negative emotions, even by means that harm them and others, such as drug or alcohol abuse. As Kelly McGonigal notes in her book *The Willpower Instinct*, when we feel bad, we desire to alleviate our bad feelings, and this can lead us to act against what we know is right.[7] We have a moral responsibility to avoid, insofar as is reasonably possible, putting ourselves in occasions of wrongdoing—that is, the near occasions of sin. Since negative emotions are often occasions of doing wrong, our moral responsibilities include a concern for our emotional life. If we often say and do things that we regret when we are intensely sad or angry, we can act better by avoiding, inasmuch as we can, becoming intensely sad or angry.

As negative emotions often draw us to doing wrong and focusing on ourselves, positive emotions can draw us outward toward connecting and contributing to others. Barbara Fredrickson has proposed the "broaden and build" theory of positive emotions. She argues that the person experiencing joy, amusement, gratefulness, or contentment is more open to the world and more likely to build relationships with others.[8] As Gretchen Rubin, author of *The Happiness Project,* points out, "Studies show that happier people are more likely to help other people. They are more interested in social problems. They do more volunteer work and contribute more to charity."[9] Our own positive emotions are not normally set in opposition to the well-being of others, for often our positive emotions can help us to be our best selves for others. Usually, our positive emotions prompt us to be more generous, more kind, and more concerned about others. We will typically find it easier to do the right thing when experiencing positive emotions than when experiencing negative emotions.

In addition, the Christian duty to love our neighbor as ourselves leads to a concern about the state of our emotions because of the impact of our emotions on other people's emotions. When we experience negative emotions, it affects all those with whom we have contact. Just as we can transmit a contagious disease to other people, so too through emotional contagion, we influence (positively or negatively) all those around us.[10] When we are "down," the people around us are more likely to get "down" too. If we want to bring joy to our neighbor, a good place to begin is by seeking joy ourselves. The woman ladling onion soup to the homeless teenage boy is more saintly if she serves the soup with a bright, genuine smile rather than with grim duty chiseled on the pursed lips of her face. He needs not just food, but good cheer.

Emotions also matter morally because we have a moral duty to take care of our own health, which can be damaged by chronic negative emotions. Since our emotions greatly influence the emotions of others, we can also negatively or positively influence the health of others in our life. Indeed, happy moods positively influence not just the life but the well-being of others. Sonja Lyubomirsky writes, "An avalanche of studies has shown that happy moods lead people to be more productive, more likeable, more active, more healthy, more friendly, more helpful, more resilient, and more creative."[11] Positive emotion is tied to positive outcomes in other dimensions of human flourishing as well.

Finally, our emotions matter because they can distort or enhance our thinking. When we are upset, for example, when we are in a "fight or flight" mode, we cannot think as clearly as when we are in a "calm and connect" mode. Since practical wisdom is needed in order to act well, we have good reason to cultivate positive emotions. As Barbara Fredrickson points out:

> Your awareness narrows with negative emotions and broadens with positive ones. It is when feeling good, then, that you're best equipped to see holistically and come up with creative and practical solutions to the problems you and

others are facing. Your wisdom, then, ebbs and flows just as your emotions do.[12]

Cultivating positive emotions can aid us in making wise decisions because when we are in a positive frame of mind, we can take a broader view of what is going on and can be more open to building healthy relationships.

St. Ignatius of Loyola, the founder of the Jesuits and the author of the *Spiritual Exercises,* made similar recommendations to those to whom he gave spiritual direction. He advised them to make decisions and changes out of a spirit of consolation, rather than desolation. Consolation is an uplifted, joyful, and happy spirit. Desolation is a feeling of downheartedness, fear, and anxiety. St. Ignatius recommended that people who are enveloped in a spirit of desolation not make any significant life decision or major change.[13] By contrast, we make wiser decisions for ourselves and for others out of a spirit of consolation.

So our emotional life matters in part because it can foster or hinder our Christian duty to love our neighbor. Positive emotions are a part of happiness, well-being, or flourishing, but positive emotions are not the whole of happiness. Positive emotions are characteristically side effects of our activities. Positive emotions normally arise from activities, a bit like perspiration normally arises from intense physical exercise. This leads naturally to Seligman's second element of happiness: engagement.

The Way of Engagement

Engagement, the second element of PERMA, is also known as "flow," making use of signature strengths in an activity requiring energized focus on the moment, an activity that is neither too difficult nor too easy. In his book *Flow: The Psychology of Optimal Experience,* Mihaly Csikszentmihalyi understands engagement or "flow" as involving a challenging activity requiring concentration on the present, which results in a sense of "time stopping" and a "loss of self."[14] The avid gardener tending her white roses, the football player on the final play of a tied game, and the jazz musician in live performance all experience flow in their activities. Flow can take place in work, in hobbies, or in sports, when the athlete is "in the zone" making use of a signature strength. In *Anna Karenina,* Tolstoy describes flow in one character's work:

> The longer Levin went on mowing, the oftener he experienced those moments of oblivion when his arms no longer seemed to swing the scythe, but the scythe itself his whole body, so conscious and full of life; and as if by magic, regularly and definitely without a thought being given to it, the work accomplished itself of its own accord. These were blessed moments.[15]

Flow is part of a happy life, and we can have flow in many different kinds of activities. Taking note of human diversity, positive psychologists hold that each person has signature strengths that fall under the general categories of wisdom, courage, justice, temperance, transcendence, and humanity (charity). Within each general category, there are subcategories that define more precisely the strength in question, such as creativity, leadership, loving and being loved, open-mindedness, teamwork, and kindness. When a person makes use of a signature strength in a challenging activity with energized focus of attention to optimum performance, the person experiences flow or full engagement.

How do Christian belief and practice fit the concept of engagement? From the Christian perspective view, God is a God of engagement. He creates the world, sustains the world, and interacts with the world. Any and all legitimate work, whether for money or freely given, can therefore be a way of imitating God, a way of being united with God. Prior to the Fall, God calls Adam in the Garden of Eden not to idleness but "to cultivate and care for it" (Genesis 2:15). In the New Testament, the call to engaged work is also present. Jesus said, "My Father is always at his work to this very day, and I too am working" (John 5:17, NIV). By his example, Jesus showed engagement by working for years as the carpenter's son, and then by working for three years in his public ministry.

The Christian call to engagement is also seen in various personal vocations to different states in life.[16] Through finding and living out a vocation, a divine calling, such as marriage and raising children or serving as a priest, nun, or brother, a person engages in an activity of service to others. As we will see later, the cultivation of particular virtues found in the Christian tradition echoes the emphasis of positive psychology on finding "flow" through using signature strengths.

The Way of Relationships

At the center of PERMA is *relationships*. Martin Seligman holds that "the pursuit of relationships is a rock-bottom fundamental of human well-being."[17] Again and again, the psychological research points to loving relationships as necessary for happiness. We can have money, fame, and power, but without love, we will not be happy. The Grant Study from Harvard University followed the lives of undergraduates for more than seventy years as they passed through the decades, in some cases into their nineties. It is one of the longest-running and most in-depth studies of human flourishing ever conducted. Its lead researcher concluded, "The seventy-five years and twenty million dollars expended on the Grant Study points . . . to a straightforward five-word conclusion: 'Happiness is love. Full stop.' "[18]

Jesus gave us this same message for free about two thousand years earlier! "I give you a new commandment," says Jesus at the Last Supper, "love one another. As I have loved you, so you also should love one another" (John 13:34). For Jesus, the most important thing of all is loving God and loving neighbor (Luke 10:27). The fundamental law of a follower of Christ is love.

A loving relationship with God is a source of strength for people of faith. As Sonja Lyubomirsky notes, "This relationship is not only a source of comfort in troubled times but a source of self-esteem, feeling unconditionally valued, loved, and cared for. Those of you who feel this way have a sense of security that others only wish for. Your belief that God will intervene when needed gives you a sense of peace and calm."[19] She notes that those who attend religious services several times a week are much more likely to report that they are "very happy" than those who attend less than once a month.[20]

Christian belief also enhances love of neighbor. The call of Jesus is a call to love *all* people. Jesus exemplified this through loving those who seemed least lovable, such as lepers, tax collectors, and criminals. He even loved those who were crucifying him: "Father, forgive them, they know not what they do" (Luke 23:34). Because no one is excluded from the love of Christ, no one is excluded from the love of a true Christian. This universal call to love greatly promotes happiness because rather than having to reserve our love (our goodwill, appreciation, and seeking of unity) to just our family, or just our friends, or just people like us, we are encouraged to love anyone who crosses our path. Opportunities to love are as common as people.

Christianity also fosters relationships through the idea of a personal vocation.[21] A personal vocation—say, to marry this person or to enter this religious order—specifies the call of love. To love everyone can too easily become never really loving anyone. We are more likely to succeed in following a health resolution that is concrete and specific: "I will go for a walk each morning just after breakfast," rather than, "I'll try to exercise more whenever I get the time." In a similar way, loving others is facilitated by concrete vows that make very specific our personal path to love. So in the marriage vow, each spouse promises the other, "I'll love you and honor you until death do us part."[22] In the vow of religious life, a priest, brother, or nun promises to serve God in a particular way and within a particular community. Having a concrete structure and focus for love makes it more likely we will succeed in having loving relationships.

The Way of Meaning

The fourth element of PERMA is *meaning*. Meaning is understood by Seligman as "belonging to and serving something that you believe is bigger than the self."[23] Although a person cannot be mistaken about a purely subjective feeling (if I feel grateful, then I am feeling grateful), Seligman holds we can be mistaken about what is meaningful. Pot-smoking adolescents may think their midnight philosophizing is quite meaningful, but when they sober up and grow up, they may come to realize if they listen to a recording of their conversation that nothing meaningful was really said. Conversely, depressive persons like Abraham Lincoln and Winston Churchill may *feel* as if their lives are meaningless, but we can rightly judge that they led meaningful lives. Lincoln preserved the Union; Churchill defended the Free World against Nazi totalitarianism. Meaning involves a connection and a contribution to something that is larger than the self: family, school, political party, country, or God.

Our happiness involves meaning because we all want to make a difference for the good. We want to leave the world a better place because of our existence. We hope that what we do influences others for the better. The thought that who we are and all that we do makes no difference and matters to no one, leads to despair.

How does Christian belief enhance meaning? Generosity—a self-giving service to others—is at the heart of a

Christian way of life. All Christians are called to contribute to the well-being of their families, their communities, and their world. The corporal and spiritual works of mercy are part of this, and so is any good work. All active members of the Church belong to and contribute to something larger than themselves, a worldwide community of faith.

Christianity enhances meaning through granting significance to even our small contributions that might—at first glance—appear to be quite meaningless. We can miss out on meaning by waiting for the grand opportunity to contribute but missing the everyday opportunities to make a difference for the better. Few of us will make headlines with our contributions. We will not be curing cancer, donating billions of dollars to charity, or establishing schools for orphaned children. So if we wait to make a difference only in such a grand way, we might make no contribution at all. But all of us have chances, not just rarely but every day, to enhance the lives of those around us. We can find meaning not just in amazing actions, but also in humble ways when we make life a little better for those with whom we live and work. Ancient saints such as Augustine and modern Christian guides such as Mother Teresa of Calcutta have emphasized that even small actions done with great love are meaningful and significant. The ultimate significance of our actions is not simply a matter of *what* we are doing, but also *why* and *how* we are doing it. To listen to someone intently, to smile at someone kindly, to help someone spontaneously—all these are everyday ways to find meaning.

I find meaning through helping one of my children (who has learning disabilities) with her geometry homework. Although we studied for the last two tests for hours and hours, both tests came back with the same grade: F. She has another test coming up this week, and we've been hard at work again. Now, at first glance, it might seem meaningless to try to help her with her geometry. She likely will fail the test again, and she almost certainly is not going to make a living using her knowledge of geometry. But if I try to help her with great love, then what I am doing has meaning and significance.

But does it really? After all, meaning is, on Seligman's view, objective and not merely subjective. Does it matter at all if I help my daughter with her homework? She is just one child. Do any of these small acts really matter?

These small acts do indeed matter because they forge our character. We cannot become a good person by doing a single good act. To become a good person we must do good acts over and over again. Our everyday activities, if done lovingly, shape us into loving persons. Whether we are loving persons matters, both to ourselves and to everyone with whom we come into contact. If we are loving persons, day to day, then everyone who encounters us day to day is influenced by our example and moved, either a bit or a lot, to become more loving.

Still, a question remains. Does any of this, even whether we are a loving person, ultimately matter? William Lane Craig sees the question of *ultimate* meaning as being tied to the question of God's existence. Craig writes:

> If God does not exist, life is ultimately meaningless. If your life is doomed to end in death, then ultimately it does not matter how you live. In the end it makes no ultimate difference whether you existed or not. Sure, your life might

> have a *relative* significance in that you influenced others or affected the course of history. But ultimately mankind is doomed to perish in the heat death of the universe. Ultimately it makes no difference who you are or what you do. Your life is inconsequential.
>
> Thus, the contributions of the scientist to the advance of human knowledge, the research of the doctor to alleviate pain and suffering, the efforts of the diplomat to secure peace in the world, the sacrifices of good people everywhere to better the lot of the human race—ultimately all these come to nothing. Thus, if atheism is true, life is ultimately meaningless.[24]

The emphasis in positive psychology on meaning objectively understood raises the question of God's existence. If God does not exist, then our actions—even large ones such as curing deadly diseases—ultimately make no difference. Everyone ends up dead. On the other hand, if God exists, and God is the God of love, then any loving action is ultimately a participation in God's eternal love. Christian belief provides hope that our lives—the large and the small contributions that we make to help others and to serve God—are ultimately meaningful. Christianity therefore enhances the "meaning" aspect of PERMA.

The Way of Achievement

The final element of flourishing in Seligman's perspective is *achievement*. He says, "Accomplishment or achievement is often pursued for its own sake, even when it brings no positive emotion, no meaning, and nothing in the way of positive relationships."[25] As human beings, we set goals and try to accomplish them. To fail to achieve our goals gives rise to a certain kind of unhappiness; to succeed gives rise to an element of happiness.

Jesus's parable of the talents points to the idea that Christians should make use of their gifts and abilities, rather than allowing laziness or sloth to get in the way of their developing their talents. It would be wrong for someone, simply out of laziness, to fail to achieve what he could have achieved with his God-given potential. The Christian doctor should try to cure patients; the Christian teacher should try to instruct students; the Christian business owner should try to supply goods and services to customers and jobs for employees.

For Christians, whatever we seek to accomplish takes place within the wider framework of love. In other words, some "accomplishments," such as that of a hit man successfully killing a victim, do not ultimately contribute to our happiness but rather undermine it. However, aside from "achievements" that are intrinsically contrary to love of God and neighbor, seeking to achieve various goals is part of a Christian's calling.

Accomplishments, I believe, come in two varieties: non-comparative accomplishments and comparative accomplishments. Non-comparative accomplishments are about achieving some goal, the achievement of which is independent of social comparison with others. Examples include running as fast as you can for three miles, learning to speak German, and writing an excellent short story. Comparative accomplishments, by contrast, are always embedded in some kind of social ranking with others. These include winning a three-mile race, speaking German better than anyone else in German class, and being awarded the short story prize in a magazine competition. Non-comparative accomplishment is a necessary part of flourishing, imparting a sense of agency and control to the person who is able to bring about the accomplishment. Comparative accomplishment can also bring about a similar sense of agency and control.

Positive psychology and Christian teaching coincide in setting forth cautions about comparative accomplishment. Positive psychology provides powerful evidence that the pursuit of happiness via upward social comparison (competing for social superiority) is likely to end in disappointment. Some people believe that happiness will be found if they can be better than others in some competition. If only they had more money, more popularity, more fame, or more power than whomever they are comparing themselves with, then they would be happy.

However, success, understood in terms of social comparison with others, tends not to last long. Robin Williams said he felt the joy of winning an Academy Award for only about a week.[26] For others, the glow of achievement is even more short-lived. In his book *The Pursuit of Perfect,* Tal Ben-Shahar writes, "On the evening of May 31st, 1987, I became Israel's youngest ever national squash champion. I was thrilled to win the championship and felt truly happy. For about three hours. And then I began to think that this accomplishment wasn't actually very significant."[27] Even those who succeed in being the very best in terms of social comparison do not find lasting happiness in their success, for they may end up competing against themselves. Sonja Lyubomirsky writes: "After *Thriller* became the best selling album of all time, Michael Jackson declared that he would not be satisfied unless his next album sold twice as many copies. In fact, it sold 70 percent fewer. Most musicians would be thrilled with sales of thirty million, but for Jackson the contrast with his earlier success was stinging."[28] The *arrival fallacy* describes the phenomenon that once people achieve their goals, the happiness that they thought would arrive and last proves surprisingly fleeting.[29] Like the horizon that always eludes our grasp, the achievement of superiority in social comparison does not bring lasting satisfaction but simply gives way to yet another goal.[30]

Christian teaching enhances happiness by warning us about such social comparison, specifically through the tenth commandment: You shall not covet your neighbor's goods. I never really understood the importance of this commandment until I studied positive psychology. I thought, "What does it matter if I wish to have what my neighbor has? Who does that harm?" It turns out that my coveting my neighbor's goods harms me because in order to covet I must first engage in upward social comparison. To covet our neighbor's goods, we must first compare our possessions to our neighbor's material goods and find that what we have does not measure up. Christian warnings about greed, especially for money, contribute to the happiness of the Christian by discouraging upward social comparison and thus preventing the needless disappointment such comparisons can bring.

In our culture, some people believe that happiness will be

found by either spending or possessing money. Many scholars in positive psychology have investigated the relationship between money and happiness. They have found that increases in wealth *do* significantly increase happiness, but only if one does not have sufficient material goods for basic living. The person who does not eat three meals a day, or sleep in a bed, or wear warm clothes is made significantly more happy by the acquisition of these necessities.

However, once a person's basic needs are met, researchers found no increase in reported happiness with an increase in wealth. David Myers points out in his book *The Pursuit of Happiness* that over the last fifty years, the average American has become much more wealthy. Americans tend to live in bigger houses, own more cars and televisions, and have greater disposable income than ever before, yet the average American reports being no more happy than the average American of fifty years ago. After the initial shock wears off, lottery winners report no greater levels of happiness than they had before winning. Fortune 500 CEOs are no more happy, and often are less happy, than average people. Almost everyone says that they need 10 to 15 percent more money to be "comfortable." As people become more wealthy, they adjust to the new level of affluence, and then they believe they need even more money to be comfortable. Those who may have been deaf to the Gospel's warnings against greed will find that the teachings of Scripture are supported by a finding of positive psychology, which turns out to be a kind of natural moral theology: We simply cannot buy our way to happiness.

The Christian way of life fulfills the understanding of happiness proposed by Martin Seligman's PERMA: positive emotion, engagement, relationships, meaning, and achievement. Religious belief and practice are associated with high levels of positive emotion. Christians are called to engage with the world by making use of their signature strengths or virtues. The fundamental Christian law is the law of love for God and neighbor, which fosters positive relationships. Christians can find lasting meaning in making a contribution to God's kingdom, which makes a difference not just now but eternally. And, finally, Christians are called to pursue meaningful achievements and to avoid traps such as greed and social comparison, as these can rob us of the satisfaction we experience when we accomplish our goals and can distract us from discovering where true happiness is found.

How Does Christian Happiness Differ from the Happiness of Positive Psychology?

Of course, Christians and non-Christians alike can enjoy positive emotion, engagement, relationships, meaning, and achievement. Indeed, if positive psychology is so wonderful, should we simply give up Christianity and embrace positive psychology as its modern replacement? As Paul Vitz pointed out in *Psychology as Religion: The Cult of Self-Worship*, some people conceive of psychology as a replacement for faith. But viewing positive psychology as a replacement for Christianity would be a mistake. Christianity does not undermine positive emotion, engagement, relationships, meaning, or achievement. Indeed, I believe Christianity enhances positive emotion, engagement, relationships, meaning, and achievement. Grace does not destroy natural happiness; grace perfects natural happiness.

"Dying you destroyed our death."

Roman Liturgy

First, positive psychology has no answer to the problem of death. Death destroys human flourishing by eliminating positive emotion, by ending all engagement, by destroying relationships, by obliterating lasting meaning, and by preventing any further achievement. Even before death arrives, the prospect of it can damage our well-being by arousing negative emotions such as fear and despair in expectation of its arrival. Woody Allen once said, "I'm not afraid of death; I just don't want to be there when it happens."[31] But most of us do fear death, and rightly so, especially if death is the utter annihilation of us and those we love. By contrast, the Christian conception of happiness is not confined to this life alone but extends to the life to come. The hope of heaven is that our loving relationships with God and neighbor do not end with death but continue in eternal life. Death destroys positive emotion, engagement, relationships, meaning, and achievement, but not the Christian conception of happiness, because Christianity offers the hope of heaven.

"The greatest of these is love."

1 Corinthians 13:13

Second, although each element of PERMA—positive emotion, engagement, relationships, meaning, and achievement—is desirable, the theory of positive psychology does not suggest any ordering of the elements. Ideally, we would like to have each one all of the time. But what if—in some concrete situation—we cannot have all the elements but must choose among them? Is positive emotion more important than engagement? If the elements conflict in some cases, should loving relationships take precedence over meaning and achievement or vice versa?

Christianity provides an ordering of these elements of human flourishing, which in turn facilitates making decisions. Although we all would like positive emotion, engagement, relationships, meaning, and achievement, loving relationships with God and with other people are the most important in the Christian view. In the words of St. Paul,

> If I speak in human and angelic tongues but do not have love, I am a resounding gong or a clashing cymbal. And if I have the gift of prophecy and comprehend all mysteries and all knowledge; if I have all faith so as to move mountains but do not have love, I am nothing. If I give away everything I own, and if I hand my body over so that I may boast but do not have love, I gain nothing. . . . So faith, hope, love remain, these three; but the greatest of these is love.
>
> 1 Corinthians 13:1–13

Although the best life would contain all elements of human flourishing, the most important thing both in this life and in the life to come is relationships: the love of God and the love of neighbor. Although feeling positive emotion is important, love is more important still. Indeed, by focusing on loving other people, we make it more likely that we will actually have positive emotions. Rather than focusing on trying to manipulate our emotions and thereby being overly concerned with them—"Am I having fun yet?"—focusing on loving others makes it more likely that positive emotions will occur as a natural side effect. Likewise, according to the Christian view, we should never "achieve" some goal or pursue meaning in a way that undermines loving relationships. The primacy of love allows us to see other elements of happiness in their proper place. It would be a mistake to seek positive emotions through drug abuse, for instance, since drug abuse undermines our ability to love God, others, and ourselves properly. This emphasis in Christian teaching on the primacy of love promotes human happiness by providing a reasoned and principled way of making decisions.

We know that all things work for good for those who love God.
Romans 8:28

Third, positive psychology is neutral with respect to God's existence, as is proper for a field of study that limits itself to what can be empirically verified. God is not a bodily, material being who can be weighed and measured. By contrast, the Christian understanding of happiness includes Divine Providence. According to the Christian view, creation is good and is governed by a loving God. Our own pursuit of happiness is part of a larger plan. Even our sufferings and missteps are part of this larger plan. We all suffer, and this is an unavoidable part of life. But the world is governed by a loving Father who only permits us to suffer for our own personal good.[32] This belief in the providential ordering of our own histories enhances meaning because even the sufferings we encounter are part of a larger, meaningful story. The Epistle to the Colossians reads, "I [Paul] rejoice in my sufferings for your sake, and in my flesh I am filling up what is lacking in the afflictions of Christ on behalf of his body, which is the church" (Colossians 1:24). Rather than being simply a useless impediment to our happiness, for Christians, suffering can contribute to making the world a better place and even contribute to their own long-term happiness. This is possible because God, in his Divine Providence, oversees the whole world of actions and interactions, including our own bad actions, ordering them to his wise and loving purposes. As Shakespeare's Hamlet says, "There's a divinity that shapes our ends, / Rough-hew them how we will" (5.2.10–11). A belief in Divine Providence provides hope in even the most difficult of situations.

Your sins have been forgiven.

1 John 2:12

Fourth, positive psychology does not address the problem of sin and guilt. The Venerable Fulton J. Sheen once wrote, "A Catholic may sin and sin as badly as anyone else, but no genuine Catholic ever denies he is a sinner. A Catholic wants his sins forgiven—not excused or sublimated."[33] When asked why he became Catholic, G. K. Chesterton famously said, "To get my sins forgiven."[34] While psychological practices can help relieve people's feelings of guilt, they cannot relieve guilt itself. The problem of an infected tooth is not just the *feeling* of pain but also what is causing the pain—the infection itself. To remove the pain but leave the infection is to leave the person in an unhealthy state. Likewise the objective guilt of sin, which is simply the separation from the love of God caused by the wrongdoing, requires not just a calming of subjective feelings of guilt but also a healing of the separation, a removal of the sin.[35] No psychologist can forgive sins, nor can any psychological practice. Forgiveness of sins requires the work of Jesus Christ. If our happiness is to be found in love of God and neighbor, then the sin that undermines this love must be removed. Sin creates disunion between the sinner and God. If God is the source of happiness, so long as this disunion of sin remains, happiness is impeded.

> *"Whoever has seen me [Jesus] has seen the Father."*
>
> John 14:9

Fifth, Christian faith provides revelation, which deepens our love. Our happiness is primarily to be found in love—love of God and love of neighbor. But love requires knowledge; and without deep knowledge, our love will be shallow. We need God's revelation to enhance our knowledge of who God is, so that we can love God more deeply. Without the aid of revelation, a purely human approach to understanding God will lead to partial and fragmentary understandings at best.[36] We might discover that some supreme Power orders the universe, but we could never see God as a loving, merciful Father. The revelation of Jesus facilitates a radical deepening of our love for God by facilitating a radical deepening in our understanding of God. Jesus's conception, birth, teachings, example, death, resurrection, and ascension teach us about who God is in a way that prophets, not to mention mere philosophy, could never do. When we deepen our understanding of God, we are enabled to love God more deeply.

But Jesus can also deepen our love for other human beings.

As the Second Vatican Council taught and St. John Paul II liked to echo, not only does Jesus reveal God the Father; he "reveals man to himself."[37] In becoming a human being, Jesus is united with each of us and reveals the deep value of each of us. Christians have, therefore, an extra motivation to love every human being because every human being—particularly a human being in need—is an icon of Jesus: "Whatsoever you do for the least of these, you did for me" (Matthew 25:40).

"I am the way, and the truth, and the life."

John 14:6

Finally, psychology—including positive psychology—cannot adequately satisfy the human desire for truth. Positive psychology makes use of the empirical method, which, in principle, cannot answer questions of ethics, meaning, and ultimate truth. Reality is deeper than we can know by means of the scientific method of empirical verification through experiments. The human drive to ask and answer the ultimate questions is a sign of the human disposition for a relationship with the ultimate Truth, God. Something more than positive psychology is needed to satisfy this desire to know what cannot be empirically verified. Since positive psychology limits itself to what can be empirically confirmed, positive psychology will never be able to ultimately satisfy the distinctly spiritual and transcendent cravings of human beings asking the ultimate questions. Because of its empirical orientation, positive psychology cannot supplant the role of religion, yet it can be a support of Christian belief about how to live and an aid in Christian practice.

The practitioners of positive psychology intentionally limit themselves to what can be empirically verified. By contrast, for Christians, happiness includes aspects that either are not or even cannot be empirically verified. All the aspects of human flourishing addressed in positive psychology (positive emotion, engagement, relationships, meaning, and achievement) are capable of measurement and quantification. In the Christian view, the most important aspect of happiness, God's grace, is not capable of measurement and quantification. A Christian account of a fully flourishing human life includes elements that are not subject to scientific verification. For example, the workings of grace are a necessary part of his understanding of a flourishing human life, enabling a person to become an adopted child of God and to have his sins forgiven. But, of course, grace cannot be measured, weighed, or empirically verified.

Although some aspects of Christian happiness are empirically verifiable, some people might be tempted to reject the Christian conception of happiness precisely because other aspects of it are not empirically verifiable. I think this would be a mistake. A sign hung in Albert Einstein's office at Princeton University read, "Not everything that can be counted counts; not everything that counts can be counted."[38] Although some people wish to limit authentic insight to what can be verified empirically, this view is self-defeating. We cannot empirically verify the claim that we should only believe what can be empirically verified. Science does not establish that we should only accept science. The view that we should only accept what can be established through laboratory testing cannot itself be established through laboratory testing. Someone may claim to find good grounds for rejecting a Christian conception of happiness, but the nonempirical nature of some aspects of Christian happiness is not such a reasonable ground.

Unhappy Christians

If Christian faith and practice lead to positive emotion, engagement, relationships, meaning, and achievement, and if they add to these things as I have suggested, then why aren't all Christians happy? This is an excellent question without a simple answer. We might amend a remark attributed to Chesterton and say that the best argument against Christianity is unhappy Christians.

One reason that not all Christians are happy is that not all Christians live the message of Jesus. Not all people who call themselves Christian are saints. They may love God and their neighbor, but they often sacrifice this love because they love something else (their fame, their money, their power) even more. Sin (undermining love of God and neighbor) in the lives of Christians undermines their happiness. The very best medicine won't work if left untaken behind the bathroom mirror. So too, the very best Christian prescription for happiness will not work unless the faith is practiced. Think of Scrooge in Dickens's *A Christmas Carol.* He may have nominally been Christian. But his actions and attitudes before being visited by the spirits reflected nothing of Christ. To judge whether practicing Christianity leads to happiness, we should not look at the person who does not put into practice the Christian faith. Rather, we should look to the person who does put into practice the Christian faith: the saint. No person is canonized a saint without joy. So one reason that some Christians are unhappy is that they lack the deep faith, hope, and love of the saints.

A second element that helps explain why some Christians are unhappy may be a genetic endowment. According to *The How of Happiness: A Scientific Approach to Getting the Life You Want* by Sonja Lyubomirsky, people have different genetic set points for happiness.[39] This can be seen in small children, some of whom are naturally bubbly, cheerful, and joyful, while other children are less so. In some cases, Christians may begin at a lower genetic set point of happiness than other people. These people would be *even less joyful* than they are now if they were not Christians.

A third explanation of the unhappiness of some Christians could be physical or psychological difficulties. Having Christian faith does not make one immune to diseases that undermine physical or mental health. If a Christian is in physical pain, positive emotion is less likely, engagement with life becomes difficult or even impossible, relationships can become strained, seeking meaning is harder, and achievements of various kinds may be impossible. If a Christian suffers from mental health issues, such as depression or anxiety, happiness will, for obvious reasons, be undermined.[40]

Christians believe that happiness is ultimately to be found in God, who satisfies the deep human desires for Perfect Truth, Perfect Goodness, and Perfect Love. Since our relationship with God, even for those who are most in love with God, cannot be brought to perfection in this life, our happiness in this life will always be incomplete, imperfect. To search for heaven on earth is to search in vain. Indeed, the insight that perfect happiness is reserved for the life to come is itself something that contributes to our happiness on earth. One way to undermine happiness is through unrealistic expectations of endless joy and perfection on earth. When we realize this will never happen, that there will always be difficulties and problems to a greater or lesser degree, we are able to escape from constant disappointment. Nevertheless, although perfect happiness cannot be found outside of a perfect relationship with God, we can have imperfect happiness now.

| TWO |

The Way of Faith, Hope, and Love

If God is the ultimate source of our happiness, how can we tap into that great reservoir of divine joy? The answer can be found in three theological virtues: faith, hope, and love.[1] These virtues are called "theological" because they are received as gifts through God's power (as opposed to acquired virtues, which are attained through human effort), and because they focus in distinct ways on God himself. Through the work of Christ, these gifts are given by God to help us in our journey to heaven, where alone we can find perfect happiness. The virtue of faith enables us to believe in God and in what God has revealed. The virtue of hope connects us to God as the source of our eternal happiness. The virtue of charity enables us to have a deep union with God that begins now but reaches its culmination in the life to come. These three theological virtues are gifts from above, rather than good habits that we acquire through our own efforts. Each is related to positive psychology.

Faith and Positive Psychology

So how do faith and positive psychology relate? Over time there have been dramatic shifts in how psychologists have considered faith and religion. Martin Seligman notes:

> For half a century after Freud's disparagements, social science remained dubious about religion. Academic discussions of faith indicted it as producing guilt, repressed sexuality, intolerance, anti-intellectualism, and authoritarianism. About twenty years ago, however, the data on the positive psychological effects of faith started to provide a countervailing force. Religious Americans are clearly less likely to abuse drugs, commit crimes, divorce, and kill themselves. They are also physically healthier and live longer. Religious mothers of children with disabilities fight depression better, and religious people are less thrown by divorce, unemployment, illness, and death. More directly relevant is the fact that survey data consistently show religious people as being somewhat happier and more satisfied with life than nonreligious people.[2]

Indeed, faith is related to positive emotion, engagement, relationships, meaning, and achievement (PERMA) in a number of ways.

In terms of emotions, faith dampens negative emotions and fosters positive emotions. In the words of one study,[3] religious belief "can compensate for lack of control,[4] alleviate anxiety,[5] and relieve stress," thereby easing negative emotions.[6] Faith fosters certain positive emotions such as elation in the glory and grandeur of God.[7] Belief in God makes possible deep feelings of gratitude for our existence because all of the world's wonder and goodness are not mere accidents of blind chance, but gifts given to us by a loving God.

I experience this sense of gratitude and elation almost invariably when visiting Canon Beach on the Oregon coast. The salt-fine sand, the chirping seagulls, and the rhythmic waves on one side run parallel to countless evergreen trees lining the coast. Haystack Rock, a brown 235-foot seastack, dominates the coast and my imagination. I know Haystack was formed by volcanic eruptions and centuries of erosion, which separated the rock from what is now the coastline, but I believe Haystack also is a large sign pointing to a Divine Beauty ever ancient, ever new. Similarly, I know the *Pietà* was formed by Michelangelo's chisel, but only an inhumane myopia would reduce the *Pietà* to *just* a chunk of marble shaped by a bit of metal, pointing to nothing larger. Faith opens us to the world of transcendent meaning and cosmic significance.

Because faith so often gives rise to such positive feelings, a person might think of faith as a kind of positive feeling. Some people believe that to be a person of faith means having a sense of God's loving presence, feeling safe in the divine care.

Although faith often does give rise to these positive feelings of consolation, these feelings in themselves do not constitute faith. People of deep faith do not always experience the positive emotions typically associated with faith. Mother Teresa of Calcutta lived for decades without the consolation of feeling God's presence.[8] To be deprived of such positive emotions is an existentially wrenching experience, but this loss of the felt presence of God does not correspond to a loss of faith.

Like the other theological virtues, faith is a *gift*.[9] When a Christian receives this gift of faith, it remains regardless of feelings of closeness or lack of closeness to God. When a person has received this gift of faith—through baptism of water, of desire, or even of blood, the person becomes an adopted child of God whether or not the person senses God's presence consciously, whether or not she is experiencing positive emotions. We might wonder whether we have received this gift of faith. Fr. Richard John Neuhaus once said, "If you would believe, act as though you believe, leaving it to God to know whether you believe, for such leaving it to God is faith."[10] This conception of faith as a gift is sturdier than the changeableness of sensed or emotional feeling of God's presence. As Alexander Pruss points out,

> Sometimes, Christians worry whether they might not have lost their faith. . . . Faith being a gift of grace, it is not possible to lose faith without losing sanctifying grace. It is not possible, however, to lose sanctifying grace but by committing a (formal) mortal sin. Therefore, faith can only be lost through committing a mortal sin. But in a serious Christian, mortal sin is very unlikely to be something done casually—it is a free and conscious rejection of God's love, after all. Faith is not, then, something one can "just lose." It is something one can *reject*, but only by a mortal sin.[11]

Felt faith and faith are not the same. Just as you can feel sick but actually have nothing wrong with your health, you can feel a lack of faith, though God's gift of faith remains, however unsensed. Indeed, feeling the absence of God is paradoxically itself an evidence of faith. Only a married woman can feel the absence of her husband, and only a soul oriented to God by faith can feel God's absence.

I find this a comforting way to think about faith, because I often do not feel God's presence. In this I am not alone. Joseph Ratzinger, who would later become Pope Benedict XVI, wrote that "the believer is always threatened with the uncertainty which in moments of temptation can suddenly and unexpectedly cast a piercing light on the fragility of the whole that usually seems so self-evident to him."[12] St. Thérèse of Lisieux struggled with atheism in her Carmelite convent.[13] Not every believer, but many, will live for a time, even a long time, in such a state.

Although faith does not always bring emotions such as gladness and consolation, characteristically faith does bring about positive emotion (the *P* of PERMA). Faith also provides the basis for engagement (the *E* of PERMA) in activities such as worship, fellowship, and personal prayer. Faith provides the basis for a person participating in these activities and so finding the focused engagement, the "flow" that arises from them. In positive psychology, spirituality, religiousness, and faith are considered "signature strengths."[14] Making use of signature strengths, particularly a novel use of such strengths, leads people to enjoy "flow," an experience of happiness.

Faith also enhances relationships. Faith makes possible a relationship with God—a permanent, lasting, intimate, and loving relationship. Beyond any human person, God is with us, communes with us, and comforts us throughout life. Christian faith also enhances human relationships by inviting us to love all other people. Rather than limiting ourselves to loving those of our own tribe, those who share our own beliefs, or those who are of our own race, Jesus calls Christians to a universal love of every single human being. In the Christian view, every single human person—regardless of age, sex, religion, or disability—is made in God's own likeness and image, so we can appreciate this image in every human person. The command to love our neighbor reminds us of the opportunities for positive relationships with whomever we come into contact.

Faith enhances meaning (the *M* of PERMA) because the person of faith sees what he is doing as making a difference not just in the short term, but also for all eternity. Seeking meaning involves making a contribution to the well-being of something larger than oneself. If people do not believe in God, then they can view their contributions as making only a limited difference, which will soon be forgotten and obliterated as time passes. Those whom we have benefited will die, and all living memory of us will be forgotten. Whatever good we do will never be lasting. Even the greatest hero (like the greatest villain) becomes, as the centuries go by, a mere footnote in a history book. Someday even all the history books will be gone as the sun expands into a red giant entirely destroying the earth.

People of faith believe that their contributions, even the small things they do, make a lasting difference. In his book *The Love That Made Mother Teresa*, David Scott expresses the point as follows:

> Karl Stern, the Catholic psychoanalyst, credited St. Thérèse of Lisieux with discovering what he called the Law of the

> Conservation of Charity. This law, he explained in his great essay on the saint, states that "nothing which is directed either toward or away from God can ever be lost." Further, he said, "in the economy of the universe," there is an "inestimable preciousness . . . [in] every hidden movement of every soul." In laymen's terms: God has so made the world that everything we do or don't do has cosmic significance. With each new moment, we are presented with a fundamental option—to direct our acts and intentions either toward God or away from him. To love or not to love. And our little decisions in these matters have spiritual consequences we can scarcely imagine.[15]

What we do now really matters, not just now, but into eternity. Furthermore, people of faith believe they are making a contribution to the most important of all projects: God's own providential plans in history. Nothing is "bigger" than that. This good news is made even better because we can all make significant contributions, since even the little things we do (which would never make headlines) can be done with great love. The importance of our contribution is principally measured by the love with which we act.

And, finally, faith enhances achievement or accomplishment (the *A* of PERMA). Of course, believers and nonbelievers alike enjoy seeking and accomplishing their goals whatever they may be. Faith opens the door to new forms of achievement, such as works of Christian charity, the development of the spiritual life of prayer, and the cultivation of the virtues.

For this reason, a spiritual director can aid us greatly on

our journey toward happiness. We need a coach to help set and reach goals in the spiritual life. These goals are often extremely practical. In the back of a small prayer book, I still have a list of the resolutions that one spiritual director helped me to strive to realize: "February 12, clean up the house each night. . . . March 12, make extra time to have fun with the kids. . . . May 3, find a babysitter to have night out with Jen. . . ." When I followed through with these resolutions, I improved my life and the lives of those I love.

Christian faith also prompts believers to set goals that are more likely to bring about lasting happiness. Researchers distinguish extrinsic goals from intrinsic goals. Extrinsic goals are sought as a means to becoming more famous, powerful, or rich. Intrinsic goals, by contrast, are sought for their own sake as rewarding in themselves.[16] It turns out that those who seek to achieve intrinsic goals are much more likely to find happiness than those who seek extrinsic goals. Christian faith aids in the achievement element of happiness by warning believers against excessive love of fame, power, and riches. These things are not bad in themselves, but if we love these things too much, we may love God and neighbor too little. Of course, Christians may make fame, power, or riches the ultimate goal of their lives, just as anyone else can, but in doing so such Christians act against the faith they claim. Christian warnings about excessive love of fame, power, and riches may serve to steer Christians away from setting extrinsic goals and toward setting intrinsic goals.

Christian belief may also help with the achievement element of human flourishing by encouraging us to seek harmonious goals. One way people can undermine their own happiness is by having goals that are not harmonious—such as making more money by illicit means and making a reputation for honesty. Christianity aids with setting goals by providing a way of ordering goals, by providing a clear structure for what is more important (love) and what is less important (money).

Hope and Suffering

Along with the gift of faith, every believer receives the gift of hope. But what exactly is hope? "Hope" is a word that is often on our lips. We hope this challenging situation turns out for the best. We hope for good health. We hope to earn more money. All of our small hopes are geared to a bigger hope, the hope of happiness, and most of all the hope of perfect happiness. The virtue of hope, as understood in the Christian tradition, grows out of faith and is a manifestation of love, since by hope we move toward a perfect loving union with God in heaven. The Christian sense of hope means trusting that God will help us to reach heavenly bliss.[17]

It is self-evident that we are not yet enjoying perfect happiness. Suffering, pain, and loss are a part of every human life. Everyone experiences both minor and major setbacks. Such setbacks can undermine our relationship with God and our relationships with other people. If God is really God—all-powerful, all-good, and all-loving—then why do we suffer?

Some people think that all suffering comes from God as a punishment for their wrongdoing. According to this view, if God really loved us or if we did not do wrong, we would not suffer. We can be like the disciples who saw the blind man and asked Jesus, "Rabbi, who sinned, this man or his parents, that he was born blind?" (John 9:2). Suffering, from this point of view, is sent directly by God to punish wrongdoers.

But surely this view is incorrect. In answering the question of the disciples, Jesus said that neither the sins of the man nor the sins of his parents led to the man's blindness (John 9:3). Although sin can lead to suffering, like when self-absorption leads to a loss of friends, suffering can also arise even if the cause is not one's own personal sin. After all, although he was entirely without sin, Jesus suffered—emotionally and physically. Jesus wept, felt sorrow unto death, and experienced the torture of scourging and crucifixion. We can compound our suffering by adding on top of it a feeling that God has rejected us. Then not only do we have the suffering that we are going through, but we also have the added suffering of feeling God does not love us. But, as the example of Jesus makes clear, suffering is not simply or always the result of our own personal sin.

Unlike Jesus, each one of us has failed to love God and to love other people as we should. We have all sinned. Doesn't God punish sin? In order to understand God's punishment, we must distinguish between artificially imposed and naturally occurring consequences.[18] Punishment consists in the deprivation of some good of which the wrongdoer is no longer worthy. Artificially imposed consequences are punishments brought about by an outside authority who creates a connection between the crime and the punishment. For example, the judge may sentence the eighteen-year-old who murders her parents to life in prison. Note *this* crime has no intrinsic, necessary connection to *this* punishment. The young murderer could have been punished by forty years in prison or by capital punishment. Indeed, the president could intervene and pardon the criminal so she receives no punishment at all. By contrast, in the case of natural consequences, the crime always naturally fits the punishment. No external authority imposes the punishment and thereby creates a connection between the wrong done and the natural consequences. The punishment is intrinsic to the transgression.[19] So the artificially imposed consequence for the person who kills her parents may be a whole range of things. The natural consequence of the eighteen-year-old who kills her parents is that she becomes an orphan with all the negative ramifications that arise for orphans.

How does this relate to God's punishment of sin? Some people think that God "sends" people to hell. They commit a serious infraction against the moral law, such as murder, and God as Judge sentences them to hell. According to this view, God creates an artificial connection between crime and punishment.

I think, by contrast, that hell is a natural consequence of wrongdoing. St. Augustine said, "The punishment for sin is sin."[20] Sin is the voluntary separation from God brought about by the sinner. If God is the source of happiness, then whenever we sin we separate ourselves from the source of perfect happiness. If our happiness as human persons is to be found through loving God and loving neighbor, people who refuse to love God or neighbor are destroying their own happiness.[21]

What is "heaven" after all? To be in heaven is to love God and to love others in God. Heaven begins wherever love of God begins. So heaven can begin in this life. As St. Catherine of Siena said, "All the way to heaven is heaven."[22] Since our love of God is always imperfect in this life, our enjoyment of God and others in God will necessarily be imperfect. So although heaven begins in this life, the full experience of heaven is not enjoyed in this life. Likewise, all the way to hell is hell. What is hell? To be in hell is to lack love of God and neighbor. Death merely reveals and confirms what was really there all along—either love or hate, either warm relationship or cold isolation. Archbishop Fulton J. Sheen captures these insights well: "As a matter of fact, heaven is not way out there; heaven is in here. Hell is not way down there; hell could be inside of a soul. There is no such thing as dying and then going to heaven, or dying and going to hell. You are in heaven already; you are in hell already. I have met people who are in hell. I am sure you have too. I have also seen people with heaven in them."[23] As C. S. Lewis puts it, "I think earth, if chosen instead of Heaven, will turn out to have been, all along, only a region in Hell: and earth, if put second to Heaven, to have been from the beginning a part of Heaven itself."[24] Lewis adds, "The Blessed will say 'We have never lived anywhere except in Heaven,' and the Lost, 'We were always in Hell.' And both will speak truly."[25] Hope focuses on these ultimate ends, gaining heaven and avoiding hell, ultimate ends that are partially found prior to death.

Whatever our destiny after death, we all certainly endure suffering in this life. As Woody Allen once said, "Life is full of misery, loneliness, and suffering, and it's all over much too quickly."[26] We also fear the suffering that has not yet come. In dark times we can imagine a future filled with even greater affliction, debilitating loss, and destroyed dreams. Indeed, worrying about what can go wrong in the future can darken the present. Some of us experience catastrophic events in which all hope appears almost extinguished. Consider, for example, those who suffered in concentration camps: physically abused, daily threatened by death, enduring the loss of all property and privacy, and mourning the extinction of so many friends and relatives. In his book *Man's Search for Meaning,* the Holocaust survivor Viktor Frankl noticed that prisoners in Auschwitz reacted to these horrible circumstances in radically different ways. Some killed themselves by walking into a high-voltage electric fence, while others praised God even as they walked into the gas chambers. As Frankl remarked, quoting Nietzsche, "He who has a *why* to live for can bear with almost any *how*."[27] We need hope to live.

Hope, in the natural order, can come in the most unlikely of guises. Our family has one of those white, fluffy dogs that was meant to trot alongside Paris Hilton, Betty White, and, apparently, a philosophy professor. Since I'm allergic to most animals, I didn't want pets in our house. So, for years my wife, an avowed animal fanatic, sacrificed her desire for a pet. I hoped the babies would make up for the loss of a pet, but she continued to debate the question for twenty years. And then one day she decided to end the debate by bringing home a dog, Lulu (I'll thank you to keep your comment to yourself). She pees on the sofa, pulls on her leash, and barks like a maniac when anyone comes to the door. She does exactly what I feared a dog would do. But she has converted me, and even enlightened me. When anyone from the family comes home, Lulu goes wild with delight. She wriggles and wiggles, licks and kisses, jumps and frolics. She exhibits pure delight at the mere fact that someone who left the house, even five minutes ago, has returned. Nothing is ever so awful that Lulu can't bring a smile to my face. Teenager caught sneaking out? Lulu still bounds through the hall to greet me. Report cards not what I had hoped? Lulu still wants to go for a walk. Kid feeling left out? I don't have to heal everything. That kid will take Lulu on his lap and within minutes be smiling in spite of himself. Lulu is like a little ball of hope. And I have become convinced that God gave us animals to heal some of our wounds, to remind us of his enduring love, and to refresh us with hope. But the infused gift of hope from God is much greater than simply uplifted spirits caused by a fluffy dog. The hope given by God to us is the conviction that no matter how hellish things are here and now, God can bring us to Heaven in the future.

How does positive psychology fit into this discussion of suffering and hope? Positive psychology, especially the work of Martin Seligman, emphasizes cultivating an optimistic, rather than pessimistic, attitude in the face of life's inevitable obstacles and disappointments. Seligman found that a person's style of explanation determines whether she is crushed and destroyed by the setbacks of life or whether she is resilient.[28] This style of explanation can be challenged and changed for the better. In the face of evils, the pessimist believes: "This setback ruins everything, this will last forever, and I can do nothing about it." Seligman devised cognitive therapy interventions that introduce alternative explanations: "This bad thing does *not* ruin everything, it will *not* last forever, and I *can* do something about it."

The Christian with the theological virtue of hope is, in

Seligman's terms, an optimist with the resources to embody resilience in the face of suffering. The theological virtue of hope seeks eternal happiness, to be achieved with God's help. In the face of even the worst of life's trials, the hope-filled Christian believes that this evil will not last forever because in the end "God shall wipe away all tears from their eyes; and there shall be no more death, neither sorrow, nor crying, neither shall there be any more pain: for the former things are passed away" (Revelation 21:4). No evil inflicted from without can ruin everything, since the hope of heaven can never be stolen away by exterior force no matter how strong. Even deadly sin does not destroy the hope of heaven, for as long as life endures, reconciliation with God is possible. Finally, a hope-filled Christian can always do something about evil. Of the deadly sin, I can repent. In the face of nonmoral evils, I can pray and work. In the face of suffering, I can attempt to relieve it and unite what I endure with the sufferings of Jesus. As Paul says, "I rejoice in my sufferings for your sake, and in my flesh I am filling up what is lacking in Christ's afflictions for the sake of his body, that is, the Church" (Colossians 1:24). The "optimistic explanatory style" advocated by Seligman is embedded in the theological beliefs and practices of the Christian.

That is why hope is the signature virtue of Christians in suffering. The American Jesuit Father Walter J. Ciszek spent fifteen years in the Soviet Gulag of arctic Siberia, cracking rocks with sledgehammers, shoveling coal onto ships, and lending support to fellow prisoners. "Men died in those camps," wrote Ciszek, "especially those who gave up hope. But I trusted in God, never felt abandoned or without hope, and survived along with many others."[29] If hope could help get him through fifteen years in a Soviet Gulag in Siberia, it can help us get through our less vigorous trials.

Love: Goodwill, Appreciation, and Unity

Although faith and hope are vital, the greatest of the virtues is love. Virtually everyone celebrates the value of love,[30] but love defies easy definition. Let's begin with love between human persons. When we love people, we have goodwill for them, we appreciate them, and we seek unity with them in appropriate ways.[31]

Goodwill, understood as kindness and generosity to others, itself induces happiness. Not only does Scripture urge Christians "to do good, to be rich in good works, to be generous, [and to be] ready to share" (1 Timothy 6:18), but researchers have found that such actions also help the ones who show the kindness. Numerous studies indicate that doing kind acts significantly boosts happiness. Kindness boosts happiness for a variety of reasons. As Sonja Lyubomirsky notes:

> Plentiful evidence for the reasons (or mechanisms) for why helping brings happiness comes from psychological theory and research. Being kind and generous leads you to perceive others more positively and more charitably (e.g., "the homeless veteran may be too ill to work" or "my brother really tries at math, but it doesn't come easily to him") and fosters a heightened sense of interdependence and cooperation in your social community. . . . Doing kindness often relieves guilt, distress, or discomfort over others' difficulties and

suffering and encourages a sense of awareness and appreciation for your own good fortune.[32]

A surefire way to increase one's own happiness is to focus on making someone else happy. In giving, we receive, as the Prayer of St. Francis puts it.

I used to think that love was simply doing good, kind actions for others. Goodwill is certainly part of love, but love is deeper than just doing good deeds. For many years, my misconception of love as simply goodwill impoverished my love for my wife. I would do kind actions for her—but what she also needed was for me to really recognize and appreciate *her*.

One day, as I was about to walk into the beautiful chapel on the campus of the Eternal Word Television Network in Birmingham, Alabama, this lesson came home to me. Just outside the chapel I saw Morgan Weistling's painting *Water to Wine*, depicting the first miracle of Jesus. In the middle of an archway, Jesus stands over two servants, directing them with outstretched arm to pour water into a massive jar. One servant gasps in astonishment as the water turns to wine just as it clears the rim of the jar. Jesus's mother, Mary, looks on in the background as people dance at the wedding reception. What does this miracle mean? It struck me that Jesus wants our marriages—indeed our lives—not merely to survive, but to flourish. Water works well enough for mere survival, but wine brings joy, exuberance, and lightness of heart. I remember praying, "God, enlighten my mind. Help me see my wife as your gift, wine and not merely water. Help me to recognize and appreciate all the good that is in her." I entered the chapel and began to write about the ways in which Jennifer is good, honorable, gracious, lovely, pure, excellent, and worthy of praise. God made her creative—verbally and artistically, a great listener, an empathetic person, beautiful, especially caring toward infants, a loyal friend and spouse. . . . I wrote for a long, long time. And then I gave the letter to her.

I too often fail to appreciate the strengths and virtues of my spouse, siblings, friends, coworkers, and neighbors. In order to improve on seeing the goodness of others, I made this beautiful passage in Scripture a part of my prayer:

> Whatever is true, whatever is honorable, whatever is just, whatever is pure, whatever is lovely, whatever is gracious, if there is any excellence and if there is anything worthy of praise, think about these things [in everyone I meet today]. (Philippians 4:8)

I had, inadvertently, discovered something recommended by John Gottman in his bestselling book *The Seven Principles for Making Marriage Work*.

Gottman, a professor of psychology at the University of Washington, has studied thousands of couples in his "love lab" in Seattle. He invites couples willing to participate in his research to spend the weekend in an apartment that has cameras and microphones recording their every conversation. He and his research assistants carefully study the interactions of the couples, looking for signs that are predictive of the future of their relationship. Gottman can predict with 91 percent accuracy which couples will stay together and which couples will end up divorced.[33] *The Seven Principles for Making Marriage Work* details what distinguishes the successful couples from the couples who later divorce. One of the key traits of successful couples is that they nurture admiration by deliberately looking for what is good in the other. He even suggests writing a letter in which you detail all the good qualities of your spouse.

Love is not merely *doing* good for others, but *recognizing* the good in others. A cold, impersonal donation to people given with disdain and contempt for them as persons is not a loving act, but merely a beneficial act. Real love recognizes the value, worth, and good of the other person. Real love, in other words, involves appreciation.

What this means is looking for the good news in others. Of course, everyone is imperfect, but everyone who is alive is made by God, loved by God, and invited by God to heavenly bliss. Such a vision is not mere wishful thinking but rather a focus on the ways, in reality, that the person is good—for example, social intelligence, ambition, strength, compassion, beauty, creativity, wit, a ready laugh, humility, generosity, social savvy, or kindness. Chances are everyone you meet will have good qualities that are easier to identify than, say, the good points of Darth Vader. Yet even the Dark Lord of the Sith is not pure evil. He is determined, intelligent, powerful, single-minded, and adept with his red light saber. All these qualities are good, albeit usually put to bad use. Anakin Skywalker loved deeply as a youth, which led to his fall. He always had within him the potential for good, and it was realized only at the very end of his life when his son recognized his potential. If even a fictional villain, depicted as an icon of evil, has some good within him, surely everyone we meet will reflect, however dimly, some good news.

In addition to goodwill and appreciation, love also seeks unity with the loved one. The kinds of unity people seek depend on the relationship and the realities of the people involved. A loving mother might seek unity with her daughter through teaching her to ride a bike, with friends in a book club discussion, and with her mother through sharing lunch. Anyone who loves wants to be united in some way with the one she loves. A disordered love seeks unity in ways that do not reflect the reality of the one we love, such as a father loving his twenty-year-old daughter as if she were still eight years old.

The Gift of God's Love

Christians are called to love everyone, even enemies. I believe loving enemies is impossible without God's help. We can have a natural love for *some* people, but to love *everyone*, even our enemies, requires help from above. Love in this sense is, like faith and hope, a supernatural gift. This gift of love is a participation in God's own nature, for "God is love" (1 John 4:8). God has *goodwill* for every human being because every person is created with God's help, kept in existence by God, and called to find happiness in God. God knows each one of us intimately, so God *appreciates* all the goodness that is in each of us. Finally, God has *unity* with each of us in knowing our hearts and in willing what is good for us, including willing that we enjoy the good of having free will so that we can will the good for ourselves. The virtue of charity, a gift from God, enables us to love others in a way similar to how God loves us. With God's help, we can grow toward having goodwill for all people. With God's help, we can see better that every single human person, even an enemy, has value, worth, and goodness. With God's help, we can move toward being more unified with others in hoping and working for the good for them and for all.

In addition to loving other people, part of the gift of God's love is enabling us to love God in return. When we love God, we have goodwill and appreciate and desire unity with God. At first glance, it would seem difficult to have goodwill for God. If God is absolutely perfect and all-powerful, it would seem that God does not need help from us in any way. However, in Christ, God becomes a human being, and through Jesus we can have goodwill for God. We have goodwill for Jesus whenever we have goodwill for a person in need. On the last day, the Gospel tells us that those destined for Heaven will say to Jesus, "Lord, when did we see you hungry and feed you, or thirsty and give you drink? When did we see you a stranger and welcome you, or naked and clothe you? When did we see you ill or in prison, and visit you?" (Matthew 25:37–39). Jesus answers, "Amen, I say to you, whatever you did for one of these least brothers of mine, you did for me" (Matthew 25:40). Whenever we love another person in need, we are serving God. Acts of love for God may be choosing to do what God would have us choose (such as loving human beings); expressing appreciation for who God is in worship; and unifying our minds, wills, and hearts with God through prayer, contemplation, and service.

Love of God is the greatest love. Since God's will is most perfect, in choosing to unite our will with God's, we know we will be willing what is best. Since God is the greatest good, in God is the most goodness to be appreciated. Finally, the most full union possible is with God, since God is always with us, always willing to communicate, and always wanting what is best for us. God is always perfectly united with us through his knowledge and love, a knowledge and love of us that is greater than can ever be had between two human beings.

Love involves a desire for unity. When we love people, we want to know them and to be united with them often through conversation. Love for God, like love between human beings, stimulates the desire for knowledge and communication. Prayer, a communication with God that deepens our knowledge of God, is the subject to which we now turn.

| THREE |

The Way of Prayer

One way to love God and neighbor is through prayer. In raising our mind and heart to God in prayer, we join ourselves to God's goodwill for all; we appreciate the Divine goodness, truth, and majesty; and we become unified with God's mind and will. Both individual prayer and communal prayer are beneficial.

In my research, I discovered interesting intersections between psychology and prayer. For example, Jesus told his disciples, "Love your enemies, and pray for those who persecute you" (Matthew 5:44). Contemporary research has shown the value of this advice for reducing aggression.[1] One study found that "provoked participants who prayed for the person who angered them were less aggressive toward that person than were participants who thought about the person who angered them."[2] The neuroscientist Andrew Newberg found that praying the Rosary lowers levels of stress and anxiety.[3]

My wife discovered this in facing one of her biggest fears.

Of the many qualities I admire in my wife, her courage is perhaps the quality I value most. Born with an anxious disposition, she has fought against fear and anxiety her entire life. She is an introverted homebody. We've gone together (with a pack of tumbling children) to Germany twice, Washington, D.C., once, and Princeton most recently. In all four locations, our living conditions were well below what we left behind. But the greatest sacrifice for her, by far, was simply boarding the flights to and from each location. When I say that my wife had a fear of flying, what I am really saying is that she suffered with nightmares and panic attacks for three months before each flight, and a month before takeoff she would be losing weight and barely conversant. A week before the flight, her hands would tremble and she would develop a haunted look. The day before a flight, she could consume no food, get no sleep. By the time we were ready to board, she was pale and weeping, almost unable to walk onto the plane. Finally, after years of suffering, she informed me that she simply wasn't going to fly ever again. "The toll is too great," she said. "It's ruining my life." Jennifer hated to disappoint me. And she hated (has always hated) "giving in." As much as she suffers from anxiety, she also suffers from perfectionism. It drove her crazy that she could not conquer this fear. So she resolved to try again. With no prompting from me, she mounted a campaign. She enlisted a friend's husband to take her on "desensitizing" flights in his small plane. On a windy day in April, a day many people would *not* have chosen to fly in a small plane, she climbed into a Cessna 172 and took off with a pilot over the Pacific Ocean, bumping up to three thousand feet. She asked the operator of a flight school if she could use his flight simulator and practiced taking off, landing, and flying a plane. A week before our commercial flight, she flew in the small plane again and came home delighted that the landing had been so turbulent. "I think I'm ready," she said. I was extremely proud of her and grateful that she had worked so hard to overcome her fear. But even I didn't know the full extent of her preparation. Later she confided that she had been going to church every day, spending twenty minutes before the Blessed Sacrament in a prayerful plea for peace of mind and body regarding the upcoming flight. "Both elements were important," she explained. "Every time I prayed before the Blessed Sacrament, God filled me with his peace. He told me that it would be fine, that he would be with me." God wants us to use our minds and the resources he provides. Relying on God means both praying and doing.

Positive psychology also sheds light on one of the central prayers of Christianity, the prayer Jesus taught his followers to pray, the Our Father. The Lord's Prayer begins not with "My Father" but rather with "Our Father." This prayer helps us recall our common humanity. We are all children of one heavenly Father who is our creator; we are all brothers and sisters in Christ, who took on our human nature. The psychologist Jonathan Haidt points out that human beings are among the ultrasocial species who seek for our mutual benefit by extending altruistic kinship relations beyond immediate family.[4] In the Lord's Prayer, we affirm that we all are brothers and sisters in one human family.

When we pray to our Father "who art in heaven," the Lord's Prayer reminds us of where we are still on earth. We need to have realistic expectations about the happiness that is possible in this life. We will never be perfectly happy in part because we can never love God and our neighbor perfectly. Paradoxically, keeping in mind that perfect happiness on earth is impossible actually makes it more likely that we will have *greater* happiness on earth. Psychologists warn that one way to decrease happiness is through unrealistic expectations. If we hope for a perfect happiness on earth, we will find ourselves perpetually disappointed.

In praying "hallowed be Thy name," we are appreciating who God is: holy, exalted, perfect. We are loving God in an act of appreciating who He is. In praying "Thy kingdom come, Thy will be done, on earth as it is in heaven," we are uniting our will with God's will. Since God's will is for the good of all human beings, including ourselves, in praying "Thy will be done" we are also having goodwill for all people, including ourselves. Loving and serving others is a sure path to increased happiness.[5] We recognize that God's will and our own will may not always align, and in such cases, we ask for God's will to be done.

"Give us this day our daily bread" is a prayer for sustenance, not excess. Note also the lack of social comparison,[6] the mindfulness of the present rather than rumination on the future or the past, and the modesty of the request. We do not pray, "Give us more bread than our neighbor," or "Give us enough bread to last a few years," or "Forget bread, I'd like a sizzling steak prepared by a gourmet chef." Focusing on life in this way—on sustenance rather than excess, on the present rather than the future, and on what I need rather than how what I have compares to what others have—is generally conducive to happiness.

Perhaps the most challenging part of the Our Father is praying, "forgive us our trespasses, as we forgive those who trespass against us." Christopher Peterson, a pioneer in positive psychology, has written that the ability to forgive is among the most important qualities that promote happiness.[7] Without long-term relationships, deep human happiness is impossible. Since human beings misunderstand, harm, and fail each other frequently, if we can't forgive, relationships will not last. (We will address the topic of forgiveness at greater length in a future chapter.)

We pray, "lead us not into temptation," because willpower can be weakened,[8] and when we put ourselves in situations in which we will be subject to temptations, over time we'll be worn down and likely give in to temptation. The Stanford marshmallow experiment offered young children a choice: they could have either one marshmallow right now or two if they waited fifteen minutes. The children who stared at the marshmallow the most as the minutes passed by were the most likely to choose to eat the marshmallow. But the children who looked away and distracted themselves were more likely to delay gratification so as to receive two marshmallows.[9]

Finally, we pray, "but deliver us from evil." Note the communal aspect again, "Give *us* this day our daily bread," "forgive *us* our trespasses," "lead *us* not into temptation," and "deliver *us* from evil." The words "my," "me," and "I" do not appear anywhere in the Lord's Prayer. One of the leaders of the positive psychology movement, Barbara Fredrickson, the Kenan Distinguished Professor of Psychology at the University of North Carolina, understands positive psychology as being fundamentally about *relationships* rather than about *individuals*, about "us" rather than "me." Even when said privately, the Our Father invokes our sense of community.

Another prayer that builds a sense of community is the Loving Kindness Prayer. This way of praying is an extended prayer of petition, a litany of intercession for the well-being of those we love. It begins by invoking those who are closest to us and then extends outward to others less closely related and then concludes with praying for all people. This prayer begins by calling to mind a person whom you love most dearly, maybe your child, a beloved relative, or your best friend. Then, keeping in mind her goodness in various ways, you pray silently for her by name: "In the name of Jesus, may Jennifer be safe. In the name of Jesus, may Jennifer be happy. In the name of Jesus, may Jennifer be healthy. In the name of Jesus, may Jennifer be filled with the Holy Spirit." The exact words may be changed, but we pray for good things such as healing, holiness, strength, joy, and friendship for individuals by name. After praying for those people who are most near and dear to us—perhaps our spouse, children, parents, and best friends—we then move to those to whom we are less closely united: "In the name of Jesus, may [my work colleague] Robin be safe. In the name of Jesus, may Robin be happy. In the name of Jesus, may Robin be healthy. In the name of Jesus, may Robin be filled with the Holy Spirit." Finally, we pray also for people we don't know well, people we don't know at all, even for our enemies. After maybe ten or fifteen minutes of intercession for the well-being of others, the Loving Kindness Prayer concludes with a final and universal intercessory prayer: "In the name of Jesus, may everyone be safe. In the name of Jesus, may everyone be happy. In the name of Jesus, may everyone be healthy. In the name of Jesus, may everyone be filled with the Holy Spirit."

Barbara Fredrickson studied this practice of Loving Kindness extensively and wrote about it in her book *Love 2.0: How Our Supreme Emotion Affects Everything We Feel, Think, Do, and Become*. She found that people who learned and began to put this spiritual practice into their daily lives:

> experienced more love, more engagement, more serenity, more joy, more amusement—more of every positive emotion we measured. Although they typically [practiced Loving Kindness] alone, their biggest boosts in positive emotions came when interacting with others. . . . Their lives spiraled upward. The kindheartedness they learned to stoke . . . warmed their connections with others. Later experiments would confirm that it was these connections that most affected their bodies, making them healthier.[10]

The positive results of this spiritual practice affect body, mind, and relationships with others. Petitionary prayers of Loving Kindness are not time wasted, but time invested to enhance physical, mental, and emotional well-being.

The Loving Kindness Prayer (or Loving Kindness Meditation as some academic researchers call it) is practiced not just by Christians but also by Buddhists. In their practice of Loving Kindness, Buddhists, of course, do not invoke the name of Jesus. How then would the Christian and the Buddhist practices of loving kindness differ? The Christian practice of Loving Kindness is interpersonal, a prayer to God, and this gives Christians an extra reason to practice Loving Kindness.

Christians believe that God is a loving Father in heaven who can hear and respond to prayers of petition. In the Christian view, the practice of loving kindness transforms not just ourselves but (through God's power in answer to prayer) also others who may even be unaware of our benevolent wishes for them. In any case, positive psychology points strongly toward the benefits of Loving Kindness practice.

Advocating another helpful way of praying, St. Ignatius of Loyola spoke of praying using the rhythm of breathing: "The Third Method of Prayer is that with each breath in or out, one has to pray mentally, saying one word of the Our Father, or of another prayer which is being recited: so that only one word be said between one breath and another, and while the time from one breath to another lasts, let attention be given chiefly to the meaning of such word, or to the person to whom he recites it, or to his own baseness, or to the difference from such great height to his own so great lowness."[11] Just as we can pray using other parts of our body, such as kneeling in prayer or making the sign of the cross, St. Ignatius of Loyola thought that our breathing could be incorporated into prayer. Generations of Eastern and Western Christians have prayed with their breath using the "Jesus Prayer." In saying the Jesus Prayer, you can time the words of the prayer to breathing in and out. On the inhale, you say, "Lord Jesus Christ, Son of God," and on the exhale you pray, "have mercy on me, a sinner."

Psychology sheds light on not just individual prayer, such as the technique of praying with the rhythm of our breathing recommended by St. Ignatius of Loyola, but also on the communal prayer of the Lord's Supper. Upon entering a church prior to the Eucharist, believers dip their hands in holy water and make the sign of the cross, reminding themselves of their baptism and reaffirming that sacrament. Research has uncovered interesting psychological effects of washing. Washing enhances optimism following failure,[12] enables people to feel less guilty,[13] leads to their holding higher ethical standards,[14] and lessens self-justifications (rationalizations) of wrongdoing.[15]

When the service begins, everyone stands in unison. As it continues, we all sit, we all kneel, we all pray in unison. This unity of the community in posture as well as in words has powerful effects. As Jonathan Haidt notes, "Synchronized moments and chanting might be evolved mechanisms for activating the altruistic motivations created in the process of group selection."[16] Such harmony of bodies, minds, and voices creates a greater sense of "we."[17] Seeing ourselves as part of the community aids us in loving others as we love ourselves.

The Mass begins as everyone makes the sign of the cross and prays, "In the name of the Father, and of the Son, and of the Holy Spirit." We believe God is not an isolated divine abstraction, but a family of Divine Persons in everlasting loving relationship with one another.[18] Through our baptism, we have become a part of this Divine family, children of God and brothers and sisters of each other in Christ.

Although adopted children in God's family, we are not yet all we are called to be. So we pray together the *Confiteor* (Latin for "I confess"). The *Confiteor* is said together in unison, but its focus is on personal responsibility:

> I confess to almighty God and to you, my brothers and sisters, that I have greatly sinned in my thoughts and in my words, in what I have done and in what I have failed to do,

> through my fault, through my fault, through my most grievous fault; therefore I ask blessed Mary ever-Virgin, all the Angels and Saints, and you, my brothers and sisters, to pray for me to the Lord our God.

Note that we do not say, "We confess" but rather "I confess." Although sin has its communal aspects, sin is fundamentally an act of the individual's choosing. In taking personal responsibility for what we do, we affirm our human dignity. We are not wolves who act merely on instinct and cannot be held accountable for our actions. We are human beings who have been given the freedom to love. In the confession of sin, we confront something that we may not want to confront—our own failures to love—but such awareness can lead to growth in love.

What effect does admitting our own wrongdoing have from a psychological perspective? Haidt suggests that we are all expert defense lawyers in our own case. We can see immediately the extenuating circumstances that excuse what we have done. We are well aware of the noble intentions that we had and the many things that we've done well. So when we have conflicts with people, we are quick to note where *they* went wrong and slow to see what, if anything, we did to contribute to the situation. Haidt notes that finding fault with yourself is

> the key to overcoming hypocrisy and judgmentalism that damage so many valuable relationships. The instant you see some contribution you made to a conflict, your anger softens—maybe just a bit, but enough that you might be

> able to acknowledge some merit on the other side. You can still believe you are right and the other person is wrong, but if you can move to believing you are mostly right, and your opponent is mostly wrong, you have the basis for an effective and nonhumiliating apology.[19]

Admitting our imperfections, sins, and faults helps us to heal relationships, to learn from the past, and to grow in the right direction.

Except for when it doesn't. In almost all cases, a sincere apology will do a relationship a world of good, but sometimes just getting out of there as quickly as possible is even better. If your newly potty-trained daughter mistakes your host's white cashmere sweater for toilet paper, you should not bother to offer an apology. (I'd like to say this is a made-up case, but it actually happened to us.) Rather, you should leave their home immediately, without making eye contact or troubling them to speak and respond to your apology. Tuck your tail as far between your legs as possible . . . and get out. It is the only way. Just send a card with some money for dry cleaning.

Kidding aside, confession of personal sin opens the door to reconciliation with not only other human beings, but also with God. Sin is a lack of proper love for God and for others. When we lack love, we lack happiness. If we do not recognize the wrongdoing in our lives, then this obstacle to happiness remains unnoticed and unchallenged. If we are not even aware of a problem, we cannot deal with the problem. Rather than remain in denial, we can confess our sins at the beginning of Mass. We can also help ourselves by confessing our sins in the Sacrament of Reconciliation. These confessions helps us face a reality that we might be tempted to ignore to our own detriment as well as the detriment of others.

At first, this emphasis on each person being a sinner would seem to be quite the opposite of a positive focus. But the humble confession of personal defects is a corrective to a disordered pride that undermines loving relationships. Pride is a term used in radically different senses.[20] Often in Scripture, pride is used to mean a disordered self-love, an excessive love of one's own excellence, a self-deification. As Jean-Paul Sartre put it, "man fundamentally is the desire to be God."[21] I am ultimately in charge: what I think, what I want, and what I desire is the ultimate standard. On the other hand, "pride" is sometimes also used in a positive sense, to mean a proper love of yourself, the lack of which would be wrong. Not only is this kind of pride compatible with love of God; this kind of pride is required by love for God. God made you as a human person, in God's own image. In virtue of your baptism, you are a child of God, even when you are like the Prodigal Son in Jesus's parable who wandered from home and found himself hungry and lonely. So we can distinguish between *sinful* pride (making an idol of our ego, replacing God with ourselves) and *healthy* pride, recognizing the reality that we are little less than angels and temples of the Holy Spirit.

Sinful pride undermines happiness in part because it rests our value as persons on something that can be taken away from us. We might have sinful pride in what we've acquired, but whatever we have acquired can be lost. We might have sinful pride in our looks, accomplishments, or achievements, but all these too are unstable foundations for happiness. Most of all, sinful pride undermines our love for God and others. It undermines our love for God because in pride we think of the goods we enjoy as unequivocally *ours* and fail to recognize that God gives us everything, including our very lives, as gifts. Sinful pride also undermines our love for others because when we are proud we look down on other people as somehow fundamentally "less than" ourselves. The confession of sin reminds us that we are all fundamentally equal. We all make mistakes, we all do wrong, and we all need mercy from each other and from God.

After confessing our sins, we ask for help: "therefore, I ask blessed Mary ever-Virgin, all the Angels and Saints, and you, my brothers and sisters, to pray for me to the Lord our God." The community of believers, the family of God, includes those physically present at church with us but also those who have gone before us, our older brothers and sisters in faith who now enjoy heavenly bliss.

For good reason, positive psychology has emphasized the importance of role models. Inspiring examples of faith move us more than ethical maxims of philosophers.[22] The Harvard positive psychologist Tal Ben-Shahar suggests, "To find the best within me I can draw on help from the best without by asking myself: What would my role model, the person I admire, do in my situation?"[23] Fredrickson recommends that when trying to figure out what to do, we not only speak with living mentors, but also "imagin[ing] having a conversation with [exemplary people] is as good as actually talking with them. So consult them in your mind. Ask them what advice they'd offer. In this way, a cherished parent or mentor, even if deceased, leaves you with an inner voice that guides you through challenging times."[24] With good reason, Catholics invoke the saints in their prayers and ask for guidance.

The invocation of the saints also helps us in our moments of temptation. When we believe other people are watching us, we are empowered to do good and to avoid evil.[25] When we become aware of being surrounded by a cloud of heavenly witness (Hebrews 12:1), the saints in heaven who can hear us and see us, we are empowered to be our best selves. We are, of course, also under the loving gaze of God, who sees us, hears us, and judges us. When we are with someone we love, we try to be as good as we can. Holy people practice being mindful of the presence of God, and they act in this awareness.

Death, Resurrection, and Gratitude

Each celebration of the Eucharist is a re-presentation of the death and resurrection of Christ. The great confessions of faith, like the Apostles Creed and the Nicene Creed, say nothing at all about the teachings, healings, and miracles of Jesus. They state that Jesus was conceived, born, suffered, and died. We too were conceived, born, suffered, and will die. The liturgy reminds us of death also through prayers for the dearly departed and in prayers that we may one day join the angels and saints in heavenly joy. Each celebration of the Lord's Supper puts us face-to-face with a reality that we might like to forget. We are all on our way to the grave.

Paradoxically, the ancient admonition *memento mori* ("remember that you will die") serves to *increase* our happiness now. In order to fight off the hedonic adaptation in which we take for granted and do not really enjoy what we have, Christopher Peterson suggests the strategy of "mental subtraction," whereby we imagine the loss of currently enjoyed goods.[26] In remembering that we will die, we engage in a radical form of "mental subtraction," which can enable us to better savor our enjoyment of all earthly goods. As the Stoics also taught, the reminder of our own mortality can serve to rekindle our appreciation of the goods that we currently enjoy.[27] If your next meal were your last, you would no doubt smell and taste it with special care. If the next sunset were your last, you would take time to really see it. And if your next meeting with friends were your last, you'd make it a time of real connection. As G. K. Chesterton said, "The way to love anything is to realize that it might be lost."[28] This is the power of negative thinking. Catholics have a long practice of doing this in meditating on the "four last things": death, judgment, heaven, and hell. Remembering the "hour of our death" is a part of every Hail Mary.

Haidt's psychological research suggests that facing death can lead to a change in values and new perspectives on life.[29] I know this was true for me. A few years ago, just three days before Christmas, as I often do, I went out for an early-morning run of about three miles. When I got home, the house was silent. Jen and the children were still sleeping. As I stretched, I noticed some tightness in my chest. I continued stretching and noticed the light pain increasing on my upper left side. I stopped stretching and focused on what was happening inside my body. As I stood there for a few minutes, the pain did not subside but increased. I went into the bedroom and woke up Jennifer, saying as calmly as I could in my state of rising panic,

"I'm having some chest pains, and I think I need to go to the emergency room right away."

We left immediately, arriving at the ER within minutes, and I found myself hooked up to heart monitors with a full medical team scurrying about me in dizzying activity. The pain was getting still worse. The doctors told me that they couldn't tell at this point what was happening to me, but that they were taking every precaution in case of a heart attack.

Suddenly, my vision shifted. Darkness began shrinking my visual field, deflating it like a balloon. I heard electronic alarms going off, and my wife yelled to the medical team that my blood pressure was crashing. In a second or two, my visual field narrowed further to a tunnel of just a few inches. "So this is what it is like to die," I thought. My second thought—not expressed in words but in a kind of powerful instinct—was that two things mattered to me more than all others: God and my family. Everything else that at times seemed so important—dollars, deadlines, and daily dramas—was revealed in this moment as really unessential. After that powerful moment, darkness.

I don't want to leave you in suspense. I didn't actually die. I had what doctors call pericarditis, an inflammation of the sac surrounding the heart. Although it was terrifying, pericarditis is not actually life-threatening. However, thinking I was about to die shifted my perspective considerably. That Christmas was the most joyful in years. The biggest gift was being alive, and being able to share the time with my wife, children, and parents. When you feel you almost lost everything, everything becomes a gift.

The Eucharist is the Greek word for "thanksgiving," and each Eucharist recalls God's gifts to us. In the Eucharist, we are presented not merely with the death of Jesus, but also with the gift of his resurrection. We remember not just what went wrong, but more importantly what went gloriously right. The suffering we endure is not the last word. Even death is not the last word. Each celebration of the Last Supper is a reminder that no matter the depths of our suffering and trials, these evils are not insurmountable and permanent. We share, by Jesus's work, the hope of the resurrection, and the final reversal of all evils, sufferings, hardships, and deaths.

We share also in a meal. In the liturgy, the priest lifts the host and prays the words of Jesus at the Last Supper: "Take this, all of you, and eat of it, for this is my Body, which will be given up for you." He then lifts the cup and prays again in the same words Jesus used at the Last Supper: "Take this, all of you, and drink from it, for this is the chalice of my Blood, the Blood of the new and eternal covenant, which will be poured out for you and for many for the forgiveness of sins. Do this in memory of me." Shortly later, after praying the Lord's Prayer together, the community comes forward to receive the Body and Blood of Christ in Holy Communion.

Communion, considered purely in terms of the psychological effects of eating, bonds people together. Susan Kuchinskas, in her book *The Chemistry of Connection: How the Oxytocin Response Can Help You Find Trust, Intimacy, and Love,* notes that eating food causes a release of oxytocin,[30] the chemical that bonds people together. Oxytocin is released when mothers nurse their babies, when couples make love, and also when people eat together. From a theological perspective, the bond between believers is strengthened in view of the greater unity each one has with Jesus present in the sacrament.

For this gift of deeper communion with God and with each other, among many other blessings, we give thanks. Each celebration at the Lord's table is also a time to thank God for the blessings in our lives, including the promise of resurrection. Despite the evident pain and suffering in people's lives, there also is always much to be thankful for, beginning with life, friends and family, and the freedoms we enjoy. In the United States, Thanksgiving is celebrated on the fourth Thursday in November, but we have the opportunity to celebrate Thanksgiving every Sunday (or every day, for that matter). We can consider all that we have been given by God, and in grateful joy give back to God our awareness and gratitude for these gifts. Each Eucharist can become like a "thank-you note" to a kind friend who has done us a great service. It is no accident that the last words of each Mass are "Thanks be to God." This brings us to the subject of gratitude.

| FOUR |

The Way of Gratitude

In everything give thanks: for this is the will of God in Christ Jesus concerning you.

1 Thessalonians 5:18

The Old Testament is filled with injunctions to give thanks: "Give thanks to the Lord, for he is good, for his love endures forever" (Psalm 136:1, NIV); "You are my God, I will give thanks to you" (Psalm 118:28). The New Testament likewise emphasizes gratitude: "First of all, then, I ask that supplications, prayers, petitions, and thanksgivings be offered for everyone" (1 Timothy 2:1); give "thanks always and for everything in the name of our Lord Jesus Christ to God the Father" (Ephesians 5:20). Jesus commanded his followers to celebrate the Eucharist, to offer a thanksgiving. St. Ambrose taught, "No duty is more urgent than that of returning thanks."[1] In my research on positive psychology, I rediscovered the importance of giving thanks from a scientific perspective.

Robert Emmons, professor of psychology at the University of California, Davis, and perhaps the world expert in gratitude research, summarizes some of the chief findings in the scientific study of the practice of gratitude:

"Experiencing gratitude leads to increased feelings of connectedness, improved relationships, and even altruism. We have also found that when people experience gratitude, they feel more loving, more forgiving, and closer to God. Dozens of research studies with diverse participant groups have also revealed that the practice of gratitude leads to the following:

- Increased feelings of energy, alertness, enthusiasm, and vigor
- Success in achieving personal goals
- Better coping with stress
- A sense of closure in traumatic memories
- Bolstered feelings of self-worth and self-confidence
- Solidified and secure social relationships
- Generosity and helpfulness
- Prolonging of enjoyment produced by pleasurable experiences
- Improved cardiac health through increases in vagal tone
- Greater sense of purpose and resilience"[2]

The benefit of practicing gratitude toward others is now a well-established finding in psychology.

Perhaps this is why I love Thanksgiving Day, and in that I am not alone. A Gallup poll found that Americans' favorite day of the year is the fourth Thursday of November.[3] Thanksgiving Day also has the fewest number of suicides.[4] On Thanksgiving, people stop focusing on what they don't have and rejoice in what they do have. Gratitude literally saves lives.

Obviously, gratitude can be defined in different ways.

Emmons defines it as "a willingness to recognize (a) that one has been the beneficiary of someone's kindness, (b) that the benefactor has intentionally provided a benefit, often incurring some personal cost and (c) that the benefit has value in the eyes of the beneficiary."[5] Each element of this definition is important. Gratitude is inherently *social* in that it always involves a benefactor giving a benefit to a beneficiary. We are not grateful to ourselves but to another person. No one writes a thank-you note addressed, "Dear Me." In addition, in order for gratitude to exist, the giver must act intentionally, typically making some sort of self-sacrifice, to bestow something worthwhile. Finally, the one receiving the gift needs to recognize it as a gift, as something good that was freely given. Gratitude also engages at least three different aspects of the human person. We *intellectually* recognize the benefit, we *willingly* acknowledge this benefit, and we *emotionally* appreciate both the gift and the giver.[6] The term "gift" is important in this context because gifts are unearned, things to which we are not entitled, things we are not owed by the giver.

Emmons distinguishes four different facets of a grateful disposition: intensity, span, frequency, and density.[7] *Intensity* refers to the depth of feeling that someone experiences for a benefit received. Two people might receive exactly the same gift (say, a visit with a friend), but one might be barely thankful at all for the gift, while the other might be profoundly grateful. *Span* "refers to the number of life circumstances for which a person feels grateful at a given time."[8] Some people are grateful for just a few things; others have thankfulness for dozens and dozens of things such as family, friends, faith, work, and possessions. *Frequency* refers to how often a person is thankful. Do we feel grateful once a year on Thanksgiving Day or many times in the course of every day? Presumably, those with a greater gratitude span also have a greater gratitude frequency. If there are dozens and dozens of things for which you are grateful, you'll likely be grateful more frequently than if you are grateful for only a small number of things. Finally, gratitude *density* refers to "the number of persons to whom one feels grateful for a single positive outcome or life circumstance."[9] Say a husband and wife have lunch at California Pizza Kitchen. The husband with low gratitude density might be grateful only to the waiter. The wife with the high gratitude density is grateful to the waiter, the kitchen help, the cooks, the people who brought the food to the restaurant, the people who grew the food, and God, who was the ultimate first cause of everything. The husband has low gratitude density; the wife has higher gratitude density.

Growth in gratitude can be in any of these four respects. We can grow in *frequency* of gratitude when we seek to become more often aware of the good things already embedded in our lives. We can increase the *intensity* of gratitude by recalling that whatever benefits we receive almost always come at some cost to the provider of the benefits. We can increase the *span* of gratitude when we remember the many good things that we enjoy. And we can grow in *density* of gratitude in becoming more aware that virtually all the benefits we enjoy involve the collaboration of many people. Milton Freedman asks us to consider a single pencil:

> There's not a single person in the world who could make this pencil. Remarkable statement? Not at all. The wood

> from which it is made, for all I know, comes from a tree that was cut down in the state of Washington. To cut down that tree, it took a saw. To make the saw, it took steel. To make steel, it took iron ore. This black center—we call it lead but it's really graphite, compressed graphite—I'm not sure where it comes from, but I think it comes from some mines in South America. This red top up here, this eraser, a bit of rubber, probably comes from Malaya, where the rubber tree isn't even native! It was imported from South America by some businessmen with the help of the British government. This brass ferrule? I haven't the slightest idea where it came from. Or the yellow paint! Or the paint that made the black lines. Or the glue that holds it together. Literally thousands of people co-operated to make this pencil.[10]

Virtually all the things that we have—from food, to clothes, to electricity, to running water—have been brought to us by the work of thousands and thousands of people. Gratitude density is awareness of reality, as is for that matter gratitude intensity, span, and frequency.

God, Gifts, and Gratitude: The Christian Difference

Belief in God influences the intensity, span, frequency, and density of gratitude. If we believe in God, we have more for which to be grateful, since something as basic as our being alive is not a mere chance happening, but ultimately the result of a loving God's providential care. Recall that gratitude requires a benefactor who intentionally provides a benefit.

Without God, our life is merely a chance accident of reproduction. In this perspective, there is no one to whom we could be grateful. If a providential God exists, however, life is a gift from above, not a pure random occurrence, but a blessing. The same point applies to other seemingly random good things in life, all of which can be seen as gifts from a loving God, for which thankfulness is appropriate.

Every time my wife had a baby, she was transformed. A sort of mystical peace settled over Jennifer with the safe delivery of a new baby. She was preternaturally calm, radiant with joy, and completely immersed in the new baby. With every new child, Jennifer would look from the baby to me, and, shaking her head, ask: "How can anyone who has had a baby not believe in God?" She later related to me that she felt that she spent the first month of every baby's life in an almost painful state of gratitude. "Thank you, God. Thank you, God. Thank you, God," she would whisper into the baby's soft head. "That gratitude completed my joy," she recently explained. "I could not have been so happy if I had not had God to thank, for it was inconceivable that no one should be thanked for such perfection."

Gratitude intensity is influenced by the motivation of the giver. If someone gives us something but we believe the person is trying to manipulate us by this gift so that he can get something from us, our thankfulness is dampened.[11] A "gift" that is understood to be a kind of bribe inspires no gratitude. Here the Christian conception of God makes a difference. Christians believe that God is personal, benevolent, and perfect. God has free choice.[12] God does not have to give anything to anyone. Indeed, God did not have to create the universe at all.

As perfectly good, God is moved only by benevolent motives in acting. God's gifts are truly gifts given out of love, not bribes meant ultimately to harm us. Because he is perfect, God does *not* somehow increase his own well-being by giving gifts to us. Since God is already perfect in every respect, Divine giving does not somehow benefit God.[13] Rather, God's blessings are entirely for the good of others. God is, therefore, altruistic to the highest possible degree. In addition, even if people give us good gifts with poor intentions, we can, as Christians, still have high gratitude intensity because we know that, ultimately, all good gifts are from God, the first cause. All these characteristics of God serve to increase gratitude intensity for the believer.

Indeed, believers are called to be grateful for all things: to give "thanks always and for everything" (Ephesians 5:19–20). Thus, even negative things are somehow part of the plan of a good, providential God. Christians believe that "all things work for good for those who love God" (Romans 8:28). This means that even the evils we endure are allowed by God because they ultimately and mysteriously *serve our own good*. In her brilliant book *Wandering in Darkness: Narrative and the Problem of Suffering,* Eleonore Stump illustrates this thesis by considering the great sufferings of Job, Samson, Abraham, and Mary of Bethany.[14] Each of them suffered in a particular way, but in each of them the deepest longings of their heart were ultimately fulfilled by God. The belief that God brings goodness to us in such trying times can help us be grateful even in the midst of suffering. Since we have more things to be thankful for, we also have more occasions to be thankful, thereby increasing gratitude frequency. Gratitude density increases as well because the benefits received from others all ultimately depend on God as the ultimate cause sustaining everything and everyone in existence.

Not just belief in God, but also belief in Christ further enhances gratitude. Part of what inspires gratitude is the belief that the benefit given to us cost the benefactor something. If someone gives us her last copy of a book, we will be more grateful than if we know she has a thousand additional copies. Jesus gives us the gift of salvation. Sanctifying grace is unearned by us, but this gift cost Jesus dearly. The cost of our salvation includes the humility of taking on flesh as a human child, the agony in the garden, the scourging at the pillar, the crowning with thorns, the sham trials, the condemnation to death, the three falls carrying the cross, the stripping off of his clothes, the nailing of his naked body to the cross, the three hours hanging between two thieves, the lamentation "My God, my God, why have you forsaken me?" (Matthew 27:46), and finally his death. The passion of the Christ leads directly to the gratitude of the Christian.

Not just the actions of Jesus but also the teachings of Jesus help to encourage gratitude through fostering humility. Jesus calls us to humility when he teaches his followers, "Learn from me, for I am meek and humble of heart" (Matthew 11:29). The example of Jesus serving the least in society—the leper, the woman caught in adultery, the tax collector, the prostitute, and the Samaritan—moves the Christian to humble service of others. Humility opens the door to gratitude by removing a major obstacle to giving thanks: sinful pride.

If we are filled with a feeling of proud entitlement, then

the good things of life are not gifts but simply what we have coming to us. As Robert Emmons puts it, "Since at least the time of Seneca, a prevailing view has been that an overly high opinion of oneself is the chief cause of ingratitude. My work has shown that the ungrateful person appears to be characterized by . . . a sense of excessive self-importance, arrogance, vanity, and an unquenchable need for admiration and approval."[15] In the Christian tradition, this character trait is called pride. Pride can sometimes be understood in a positive sense, as recognizing the goodness that God has put into our lives. But pride in the disordered sense of the term is an obstacle to gratitude. Proud or narcissistic people feel no gratitude because they act as if everything that they enjoy is the result of their own work or something to which they are entitled. When good things happen to us (e.g., we succeed in something), we are often more apt to attribute this to our own merits or our own doing. When bad things happen (e.g., we fail in something), we are sometimes more likely to attribute this to an external cause rather than our own contributions.[16] The self-preoccupation of narcissists blinds them to the good intentions of others and the good gifts they have received. The narcissist refuses to acknowledge dependence on others or indebtedness to others, but only feels a sense of entitlement. As Emmons notes, "If one is entitled to everything, then one is thankful for nothing."[17] For good reason, pride is listed among the seven deadly sins because pride kills gratitude.

As a remedy to disordered pride, the positive psychologist Paul Wong provides a helpful list of practices for cultivating the virtue of humility:

- Acknowledging our wrongdoing
- Receiving correction and feedback graciously
- Refraining from criticizing others
- Forgiving others who have wronged us
- Apologizing to others we have wronged
- Enduring unfair treatments with patience and a forgiving spirit
- Thinking and speaking about the good things of other people
- Rejoicing over other people's success
- Counting our blessings for everything, good and bad
- Seeking opportunities to serve others
- Being willing to remain anonymous in helping others
- Showing gratitude for our successes
- Giving due credit to others for our successes
- Treating success as a responsibility to do more for others
- Being willing to learn from our failures
- Assuming responsibility for our failures
- Accepting our limitations and circumstances
- Accepting the social reality of discrimination and prejudice
- Treating all people with respect regardless of their social status
- Enjoying the lowly status of being an outsider and a nobody.[18]

These recommendations are embodied in the Christian practices of receiving openly fraternal correction, acknowledging our sins, and relying on God, as well as in the injunction to love all people.

The benefits of cultivating humility are not limited simply to enhancing gratitude. The psychologist Pelin Kesebir lists some of the research findings: "Humility has been related to forgiveness, generosity, helpfulness, better social relationships, and excellence in leadership; and found to be negatively associated with some less desirable personality traits such as neuroticism and narcissism."[19] Humility is a realistic and grounded attitude toward the self, seeing the self in the larger reality. Kesebir writes, "Humility involves a willingness to accept the self's limits and its place in the grand scheme of things, accompanied by low levels of self-preoccupation."[20] Humility not only increases gratitude; it benefits the humble person in myriad ways. To be humble, from the Latin word *humilis,* means to be inclined to the earth. The humble person is the grounded person, the one living in reality. The grounded person, much more than the proud person, recognizes the bountiful gifts of life.

Strategies for Increasing Gratitude

Three Blessings Exercise

One of the first practices that I learned about in positive psychology is called the "Three Good Things" or the "three blessings" practice. The Three Good Things exercise is simple. At the end of the day, think over what went well from the time you got up until evening. It could be that nothing major happened that day, so don't forget to look for the little blessings of life. Perhaps you enjoyed a good cup of coffee in the morning or a nice warm shower. Perhaps the commute to work took place without hassles. At work, a colleague greeted you cheerfully and you had a great chat. The sandwich, orange, and BBQ chips you had for lunch were filling and tasty. You noticed something interesting on Facebook. Once you think of three good things that happened, you simply write them down in a sentence or two and then reflect on why these good things happened. This practice is simple and powerful.

Here is an example of how this looked in my life. On the first day, I wrote: "(1) I enjoyed helping my daughter with her homework. This happened because she needed help. (2) I got some good writing done because I made time first thing for it. (3) I helped Jen fix the phone and Internet because they were not working right." These are not dramatic things to be grateful for, but they are three positive things nonetheless. The next day I wrote, "(1) I'm grateful that my daughter's visit to the doctor went well. This happened because Jen noticed she wasn't feeling well and took her. (2) I'm happy that my syllabus for class is almost done, because I worked on it a lot today. (3) I'm grateful that I had the chance to sleep extra today because I made time for it." I continued, as instructed, for seven days. Nothing during this time was dramatically or amazingly good. The good things were small, everyday blessings like the examples I've shared. Yet, amazingly, I did begin to feel different. As everyday and undramatic good things would happen (like enjoying a tasty cheeseburger), I began to notice the good, savor it, and be grateful. Indeed, what is everyday and undramatic for me (eating a cheeseburger) would be lifesaving to the millions of people around the globe who do not have sufficient food.

My experience of finding increasing happiness through the practice of writing down good things is not unusual. Just as researchers test medications against placebos, so too they have investigated the effects of the Three Good Things or blessings exercise extensively in double-blind research studies. In her book *The How of Happiness*, Sonja Lyubomirsky reports:

> In one study, the University of Pennsylvania Professor Martin Seligman taught a single happiness enhancing strategy to a group of severely depressed people—that is, those whose depression scores put them in the most extremely depressed category. Although these individuals had great difficulties even leaving their beds, they were instructed to log onto a website and engage in a simple exercise. The exercise involved recalling and writing down three good things that happened every day—for example, "Rosalind called to say hello," "I read a chapter of a book my therapist recommended," and, "The sun finally came out today." Within fifteen days, their depression lifted from "severely depressed" to "mildly to moderately depressed," and 94% of them experienced relief.[21]

In my own experience with this practice, I've found that it does reliably improve life satisfaction.

Why does the three blessings practice work? It works in part because it corrects our inherent negativity bias. What I mean is that we tend to remember negative events and to be more aware of negative events than positive ones. Reflecting this bias, we remember the unkind words of others but quickly forget compliments. Thousands of years ago, we had to be hyperaware of threats in our environment if we were to survive. Our very existence depended on seeing threats before we were attacked. Noting threats had to take priority over noticing good things. We could survive if we did not see the fruit hanging from a particular tree, but we might not survive if we missed seeing the bobcat in the tree. In ancient times, survival required hypervigilance about such threats. But today, hopefully, we are not in circumstances in which hypervigilance about threats is necessary for our survival. Yet we still have this orientation to be more aware of the negative than the positive. Psychologists calls this the human "negativity bias."

Because of the human negativity bias, we tend to overlook and not even see the good things that are in our lives. In general, what we are looking for powerfully shapes what we see. If we are focusing intently on something, we may entirely miss something else, even something extraordinary.

A most dramatic demonstration of this idea was offered by Christopher Chabris and Daniel Simons in their book *The Invisible Gorilla*. They constructed a short film of two teams passing basketballs, one team wearing white shirts, the other wearing black. The viewers of the film are instructed to count the number of passes made by the team in white, ignoring the team in black. This task is difficult and completely absorbing. Halfway through the video, a woman wearing a gorilla suit appears, crosses the court, thumps her chest, and moves on. The gorilla is in view for nine seconds. Many thousands of people have seen the video, and about half of them did not notice anything unusual. It is the counting task—and especially the instruction to ignore one of the teams—that causes the blindness. No one who watches the video without that task would miss the gorilla.[22]

What we see is influenced by what we are looking for. Given the negativity bias inclining us to look for what is wrong in our lives, we may miss an invisible gorilla in our own lives; namely, we may miss the fact that most of the time we have much for which to be grateful.

The Three Good Things exercise helps correct our negativity bias. Yes, of course, there are things in our lives that we wish were different—things about ourselves, things about others, things about our society. Yet to have an accurate and unbiased understanding we also need to recognize the good things in ourselves, in others, and in society that we can so quickly forget or even fail to notice altogether. Once we have practiced the Three Good Things exercise for a week or more, we begin to see things with new eyes. As good things happen, we become more aware they are happening. As good things are happening, I've found myself even thinking, "I wonder if this good thing will make it into my top three things for today?" Indeed, most of us live lives that are more comfortable and better than what a king in the ancient world could expect. No Pharaoh, no Caesar, and no King of France had antibiotics, cell phones, or Novocain at the dentist. Unfortunately, it is not just people in centuries past who have had to do without modern medicine, technology, and pain relief. Even in our own times, millions and millions of people lack basic necessities such as clean water and food. Whatever our material well-being, we have innumerable goods to be thankful for, but we may not even notice them. Practicing counting at least three blessings every day can help us notice the amazing blessings already present in our daily lives.

The idea of counting one's daily blessings is not, of course, the invention of contemporary positive psychology. Contemporary researchers can now investigate this practice using the empirical methods of modern science, but the practice is much more ancient. The founder of the Jesuits, St. Ignatius of Loyola (1491–1556), recommended to those seeking his guidance in spiritual direction that they practice the "Examen" every day. Certain aspects of the Examen are similar to the Three Good Things exercise. The prayer begins with seeking an awareness of all the gifts God has provided, either directly or through the mediation of other people, to us in the previous twenty-four hours. We look for God's work in our lives, and, in particular, we seek to become aware of the blessings God has given us. The next stage in the Examen is to consider how we have responded to what God has given us and whether we can grow in our love for God and neighbor. The Examen concludes with asking God's help to grow in gratitude and in love for him and for others.[23]

Fasting as a Path to Increased Gratitude

The Christian practice of fasting is also related to thankfulness. In his book *Thanks! How the New Science of Gratitude Can Make You Happier*, Robert Emmons notes: "Professor Michael Zigarelli of Messiah College has found that there is a positive relationship between periodic fasting and gratitude. He reports that people who have higher levels of gratitude are much more likely to fast regularly than are those who score lower on a standard measure of gratitude."[24] This finding may be related to the fact that whatever is scarce we find more valuable and appreciate more. I found this to be true in my own case. On Ash Wednesday, the beginning of Lent, all Catholics are called to fast—that is, to eat only one full meal and then if necessary two other meals that taken together are less than a full meal. So last Ash Wednesday, rather than having a normal lunch, I had only a bag of pretzels. Although I'd typically scarf down a bag of pretzels in minutes, this time I put a single pretzel in my mouth and savored it. Once the salt was gone, I ate it very slowly. Then, after a few minutes, I put another pretzel in my mouth, waited until all the salt was dissolved, and then slowly ate it. I've never enjoyed a bag of pretzels more in my life. Since food was scarce, I savored every granule of salt on each pretzel. Fasting leads to savoring, savoring leads to greater appreciation and happiness. It also leads to remembering with compassion the millions of people who lack even clean water to drink, let alone a pretzel to eat. The Christian injunction to fast is not then a rejection of happiness, but (paradoxically) a means to increasing happiness.

The Gratitude Letter

Another strategy to increase gratitude is to write a gratitude letter. The task is simple. Think about someone in your life who has greatly benefited you and write him a 250-word letter. If possible, visit him and read the letter to him. When I first heard of the gratitude letter, I knew immediately the person I should thank. It was my most important professor from graduate school, and I had just learned that he had been diagnosed with cancer. I sent this gratitude letter to him, and it turned out to be our last communication.

Dear Ralph,

In this month of your retirement, after 53 years as a professor at the University of Notre Dame, I thought that now would be a perfect time to thank you for the many wonderful things you've done for me since I first met you in 1992 as a student new to Notre Dame.

I really appreciate that you chose me to be your teaching assistant for your course The Thought of Aquinas, which was—believe it or not—my first course in Thomistic thought. I learned in that class and also in your many books a great deal about the relationship of faith and reason, about language, about ethics, and about God. It was there I first heard the words of the French writer Leon Bloy, "There is only one tragedy in life: not being a saint."

You also taught me so much by how you treated me. I remember the many times you took me to lunch at the Notre Dame Faculty Club and for Chinese food at the Great Wall. I remember your door being open virtually every afternoon for me and anyone else who had questions or concerns.

Ralph, it goes without saying how grateful I am to you for directing my dissertation. You directed more Notre Dame PhDs than anyone else in history, and I am so fortunate to be able to count myself among them.

Add to that the many invitations to Thomistic Summer Institutes at the University of Notre Dame during so many summers. Add to that the sage advice on many matters, and add to that most importantly your example: scholar, teacher, writer, family man, person of faith. When I think about how I hope to live the rest of my life—you are the model.

Thank you, Ralph, thank you so much.

Love, Chris

Researchers have found that writing and sending gratitude letters dramatically increases happiness. A Harvard Medical Report noted that Dr. Martin E. P. Seligman, the psychologist from the University of Pennsylvania whom I mentioned earlier in the book, "tested the impact of various positive psychology interventions on 411 people, each compared with a control assignment of writing about early memories. When their week's assignment was to write and personally deliver a letter of gratitude to someone who had never been properly thanked for his or her kindness, participants immediately exhibited a huge increase in happiness scores. This impact was greater than that from any other intervention, with benefits lasting for a month."[25]

Gratitude Journal

A final recommendation for increasing thankfulness is keeping a gratitude journal. The challenge is to write a little bit each day about the blessings that have come in life. The challenge is not just to find the time to reflect but also to keep the practice fresh and meaningful. Robert Emmons, in his book

Gratitude Works!: A 21-Day Program for Creating Emotional Prosperity, suggests having a different focus on each day and noticing details.

Mondays are dedicated to thinking about ways in which we've received gifts from others and how we might respond in gratitude. In this category, I wrote one day about my parents, who have given me so many gifts, material and nonmaterial, that I cannot even count them. Among those for which I am especially grateful: the gift of adopting me (even though I looked pretty bad as a baby), of raising me as a Catholic, of being patient with me through all stages of life (especially when I was a teenager), of giving me a wonderful education, of giving me what I really, really wanted at different stages of life (a bike, a letterman jacket, a trip to Rome to study Latin). They love Jen and the kids and show this in many ways. Next to God alone, my parents have given me more than anyone, and they continue to give. How can I respond in gratitude to them? Perhaps the best way is to try to be the best parent I can be as a way of passing on the blessings that they've given to me.

Tuesdays are meant to recall a good that is going to end soon. It could be a friend who is moving away, a job that is coming to an end, or a child who is moving out. On one Tuesday, I wrote about someone named Doris Guth, my wife's grandma. She is ninety-six years old and just took a bad fall, breaking her leg. That fall will ultimately end her life. She has given me a great deal by giving birth and raising Shirlee, who gave birth and raised Jennifer. Doris's good example in being a wife, mother, and person of faith shaped Shirlee, who in turn shaped Jennifer. Doris used to fall asleep listening to tapes of Archbishop Fulton J. Sheen, organized prayer circles, and brought Jennifer to Mass when she was a girl. Doris had a challenging life, but her faith helped her deal with these many challenges. She was always and unfailingly kind to me. I can never recall having a single cross word with her. She was always appreciative of any gifts or help that I gave. She also was so positive about my work and what I was doing. I am grateful to her for being such a good grandmother to Jennifer. They share a special kind of love. And now her long, long life is almost over. She will die, almost certainly, before the month is over. She'll return to the God who made her and loved her. She'll be reunited with all her friends who have gone before her, leaving her alone now for so many years. She'll be united with her husband who died twenty-two years ago, with her daughter who proceeded her in death, with all her siblings, with her own parents and grandparents. I hope they will all be praising God forever and ever, and praying for us who remain behind still journeying toward our eternal destiny. Her journey is now almost entirely complete. I am grateful for a great good that is now passing away—Doris Guth.

On Wednesdays, we consider the absence of blessing—that is, the fact that the good things in our life very easily could have never happened. Imagine if you'd never met your best friend. How would your life be different? What would have happened if you had been hit by a car as child and were confined to a wheelchair? Think of other blessings in your life: family, possessions, education, faith, and friends. Any one of these things, all of these things, could very easily be missing from your life. The first time I did this exercise I thought about my education. What would have happened if I had not gotten into the University of Notre Dame? This very nearly happened. As an undergraduate, I applied to ten graduate programs and got into nine of them. I was waiting for my letter from the University of Notre Dame, my first choice. Finally, the letter arrived. "I'm sorry to inform you," the letter from the graduate director read, "but we are unable to offer you admission to our graduate program." As I walked home, I thought of my second choice, the University of Toronto. I'd have to find thousands of dollars for tuition and thousands more to afford to live there while I attended school. I said some Hail Marys as I walked. When I arrived back at the dorm, I got a phone call, "Hello, this is the director of the graduate program at the University of Notre Dame. Despite our letter, we now do have a spot in our graduate program for you. We are able to offer you a full tuition scholarship and a $10,000 stipend for living expenses. Would you like to think about our offer and call us back?" Sure, I thought about it—for a millisecond. Not just financially, but in every respect the University of Notre Dame was a huge blessing—and it nearly didn't happen. Without Notre Dame, I would have probably never studied St. Thomas Aquinas in any serious way. I would not have gotten to know so well wonderful people such as Ralph McInerny, David Solomon, Randy Smith, and Jeanne Heffernan (Schindler). I wouldn't have been able to go to Germany for my postdoc. I would not be so devoted to Notre Dame football. My education would have been more narrow (just philosophy) rather than broad (patristics, moral theology, Latin). I would have been much less likely to get a job, and I wouldn't have the wonderful alumni connections I have. And ultimately I would not have done so well in my career, and more importantly in life. When we consider the absence of blessings, we remember that the gifts that we enjoy are fragile and very well might never have been.

Thursdays are devoted to considering to whom we are grateful and for what. If we think about it, numerous people contribute to our well-being in important ways, and we can recall and focus on these people and the gifts they have given us. For example, one day I wrote that I am thankful to Tom and Teresa Syta for inviting our family for a nice dinner and drinks with another family, for a night of socializing. They went to a great deal of trouble and expense to provide us with such a nice meal: food costs, food prep time, drink costs, and opportunity costs. They've done this several times. I am thankful also for their excellent example of parenting and living a life of faith.

Fridays are dedicated to writing about times in which something bad eventually led to something good. In this exercise, we look for a "resurrection" following a "crucifixion." Sometimes the good may be difficult to see. After defeating the Nazis and saving Britain in World War II, Churchill lost his bid for reelection as prime minister. His wife, Clementine, tried to console him: "Winston, this could be a blessing in disguise." Churchill replied, "If this is a blessing, it is certainly very well disguised."[26] Nevertheless, very often we can find blessings in difficulties that we have endured. Robert Emmons tells the story of a man marooned alone on a desert island:

> Each day he prayed for rescue but none came. With much weary effort, he built a hut to live in and to store provisions. Then one day the hut burned down. He cried out, "All is

> gone—God, how could you do this to me!" The next day a ship came to rescue him. He said, "How did you know I was here?" The reply was, "We saw your smoke signal."[27]

God often does bring something good to us out of something bad. God sometimes brings good even from the injuries we suffer because of the harmful choices of other people. One of those good things is the great good of forgiveness, the subject of the next chapter.

| FIVE |

The Way of Forgiveness

As the Lord has forgiven you, so you also must forgive.

Colossians 3:13, ESV

The teachings of Christ on forgiveness could not be much more clear and emphatic. When Jesus taught his disciples how to pray, he linked God's forgiveness of us with our forgiveness of others: "If you forgive others their transgressions, your heavenly Father will forgive you. But if you do not forgive others, neither will your Father forgive your transgressions" (Matthew 6:14–15). The centrality of forgiveness is emphasized in every Gospel, in every liturgy, and in every "Our Father." Even as Jesus was dying on the cross, he gave an example of forgiveness, praying, "Father, forgive them, they know not what they do" (Luke 23:34). Jesus, in his actions and in his teaching, emphasized the importance of forgiving other people—not just seven times, but seventy times seven, symbolizing a perfect, unlimited number of times (Matthew 18:22).

Christopher Peterson, a pioneer in positive psychology, has written that the ability to forgive may be the most important factor for happiness. "Forgiveness undoes our own hatred and frees us from the troubled past. Indeed, forgiveness has been described as the queen of the virtues—that is, those who forgive are much more serene than those who do not and display many other positive strengths."[1] Since human beings misunderstand, harm, and fail each other regularly, without forgiveness, human relationships will not last. If we lack long-term relationships, deep human happiness is impossible. In addition to undermining relationships, unforgiveness also sabotages the positive emotions that are part of flourishing. "Unforgiveness can be defined as delayed negative emotions, involving resentment, bitterness, hostility, hatred, residual anger and residual fear."[2] Unforgiveness actually stresses the body into experiencing an ongoing "fight or flight" response that undermines sleep, digestion, cardiovascular heath, and the immune system. By contrast, researchers have discovered that "forgiving people are less likely to be hateful, depressed, hostile, anxious, angry, and neurotic. They are more likely to be happier, healthier, more agreeable, and more serene."[3] Positive psychology provides empirical confirmation of one of the most central of Jesus's teachings: the importance of forgiveness.

Both faith and reason suggest the signal importance of forgiveness. We know forgiveness when we feel it, but how could forgiveness be defined? In order to answer this question, the Christian psychologist Everett Worthington clears away some common misunderstandings about forgiveness.[4] Forgiveness is not *forgetting* what happened. Although people often say, "Forgive and forget," this is not always possible. If the offense is painful and extraordinary, it will probably never be forgotten. If someone murders your mother, you will never forget it.

Forgiveness also does not necessarily mean that one reconciles with the person who caused the pain. Ideally, reconciliation and restoration of the prior relationship does take place with forgiveness. However, in some cases, reconciliation with the offender is either impossible because the person has died or unwise because the person is dangerous. If a business partner swindles you out of money, you may have no obligation to continue as business partners. Reconciliation requires trust on both sides, and sometimes trust cannot or should not be extended to someone. Forgiveness, by contrast, can be done by one person without the cooperation of the offender. Forgiveness can be done without a restoration of the prior relationship.

Forgiveness does not mean pretending that nothing wrong was done. Murder, theft, and the like are always wrong, and forgiveness does not deny this important truth. Forgiveness is not lying or pretending that evil actions are not really evil. Indeed, forgiveness is needed precisely because some action was offensive and wrong.

Finally, forgiveness does not mean forgoing justice. Forgiveness is a personal matter that happens within the forgiving person. Justice is always an interpersonal matter, having to do with the interactions of two or more persons. Justice as a civil and legal matter is the responsibility of those—such as judges and police officers—who are charged with defending the common good from wrongdoers. In order to preserve public order and peace, those with responsibility for the common good must administer justice to those who harm the common good; they deprive convicted criminals of goods (such as their money or their freedom) of which the wrongdoers are no longer worthy. Without contradiction, we can both forgive the wrongdoer and cooperate with law enforcement in bringing a criminal to justice.

So if forgiveness is not forgetting, reconciling, pretending, or forgoing justice, what is forgiveness? Worthington distinguishes *decisional* forgiveness from *emotional* forgiveness. Decisional forgiveness is the choice to forsake revenge. Decisional forgiveness is the intentional resolution to forgo carrying out vengeance and to behave humanely toward the person who caused the offense. Emotional forgiveness involves actually no longer having the negative emotions of bitterness, hostility, hatred, anger, and fear toward the person who did wrong. We reach emotional forgiveness when the negative emotions are replaced with positive emotions.

How can we go about achieving decisional forgiveness or emotional forgiveness? Forgiving someone is something like losing weight. We may know we should do it, but exactly how to get from where we are now to where we would like to be is often difficult. We can say the words "I forgive you," but real forgiveness involves more than just saying words. Fortunately, contemporary psychology has important insights about forgiveness and even suggests concrete steps to take to reach forgiveness.

When people are asked about how much they are hurt by the wrongdoing of others, an interesting pattern emerges. People who are resentful about major catastrophes, such as the murder of a family member, will say, "My hurt is around an 8.9 on a scale of 1 to 10." And people who are resentful about a much smaller matter, such as a boss being unfair to them at work, when asked about their level of hurt will typically say, "My hurt is around 8.7 on a scale of 1 to 10." It seems that the perceived level of suffering from an injustice does not depend so much on the true nature of the offense (obviously, objectively speaking, the murder of one you love is a much more severe harm than enduring rudeness from a boss). Rather, whatever the offense against us, regardless of its nature, it seems to us at the time to be a major offense.[5]

When we are resentful and angry toward those whom we do not want to forgive, it does not harm the person who caused the offense; it harms us. Physiologically, we experience at a low level, if not a high level, the "fight or flight" response. For a short time, this kind of response may help us deal with a crisis. If someone breaks into your house to harm you, having adrenaline surging through your body helps you tremendously if you need to flee from the intruder or to confront the intruder. But the human body was not made to be in a continuous "fight or flight," urgent response mode. Unfortunately, long-term resentments tax the body by placing it in an ongoing and endless "battle mode" in which we plot revenge against our enemy (who may not even be aware of our resentment). Long-term unforgiveness undermines both mental and physical health, not to mention emotional well-being.

So how can we move from resentment toward others to forgiveness? This question has been the subject of ongoing research by scholars around the world. One of the leading experts in forgiveness research is Dr. Fred Luskin, the cofounder and director of Stanford University's Forgiveness Projects. He has worked with families in Northern Ireland whose children were killed in "The Troubles" between paramilitary groups, as well as with other people who have experienced devastating violence. In his book *Forgive for Good: A Proven Prescription for Health and Happiness,* Luskin describes how he helped parents who had lost children on opposite sides of the Irish conflict to come together, find forgiveness, and move past the seemingly unending vendettas on both sides.

In order to shift our bodies out of the fight or flight response of unforgiveness, Luskin recommends slowing down our breathing and breathing more deeply. When we consciously regulate our breathing to be slower and deeper, we are signaling our entire body to relax, to let go, and to experience calm. As we slow our breathing, he recommends also calling to mind someone whom we deeply love so that we will experience a sense of gratitude and peace.

Once we are in a physiological state that is less "fight or flight" and more "calm and connect," we become better prepared to move toward forgiveness. Part of forgiveness is finding a new narrative to describe what happened to us so that we can react to what happened in a new way. When we are unforgiving, we tell ourselves the same story, replaying in our minds the offense, and experiencing again the loss, anger, sadness, and desire for revenge. To achieve forgiveness, we need a new story to replace the old narrative of unforgiveness.

Luskin calls his process of working toward forgiveness the HEAL method, an acromyn standing for hope, educate, affirm, and long-term commitment. The HEAL method arises out of rational emotive behavior therapy, which seeks to help people take responsibility for their own emotional reactions and to be realistic about the limitations of human beings. We usually don't have much control over our initial emotional reactions to what happens when something goes wrong for us, but we do have greater power over what happens to us emotionally later. In an article in *Stanford Magazine*, Joan O'C. Hammilton describes Luskin's insights:

> Initially, a grievance story is simply one's version of what happened. But over time, it can become something more malignant—a detail-packed, often obsessively repeated, subtly or not-so-subtly distorted account that embellishes the role of a villain who is responsible for one's misery. "The problem with our stories is they always focus on 'them'—the other person—and why he won't change or what she won't do. That gives them power they shouldn't have," Luskin says.[6]

The old story of unforgiveness reinforces an "I am a victim" identity. The new story of forgiveness needs to emphasize the reality that we *do* have control over how we frame, interpret, and react to the events in question. As concentration camp survivor Viktor Frankl pointed out in his classic book *Man's Search for Meaning*, "Everything can be taken from a man but one thing: the last of the human freedoms—to choose one's attitude in any given set of circumstances, to choose one's own way."[7] We often cannot choose what happens to us, but we can always choose how to relate to what happens to us.

Everyone has heard of the homeless Vietnam vet with post-traumatic stress syndrome, but a vet may also have post-traumatic growth syndrome. Post-traumatic growth can mean greater appreciation of life, increased spiritual understanding, increased closeness with others, and a greater sense of individual strength. Trauma can lead to positive change.[8]

A second element of rational emotive behavior therapy emphasizes the universal limitations and weaknesses of human beings. Any hurts that we've experienced, even the very worst of them, has been experienced by millions and millions of other people. Hammilton writes:

> Rotten things are happening all the time to people—marriages are failing, spouses are being unfaithful or abusive, stepchildren are acting out, business partners are being unscrupulous. To assume that because you are hurting from one of these experiences, there is something wrong with you, is ludicrous. And focusing your attention on the affront and the offender, or on how stupid you were for being duped or abused, gives the offender a power over you that is inappropriate and harmful.[9]

When we are realistic about the challenges of life, our own negative experiences will not seem so unique and so isolating. If we expect that our desires will always be met, that no one will ever treat us inappropriately, and that perfect justice will reign on earth, our expectations will be perpetually disappointed. By contrast, a realistic appraisal of human affairs suggests that we will have unmet desires, at least sometimes people will not treat us in ways we would like to be treated, and perfect justice will never be realized on earth. Christian theology has emphasized this truth by its teaching about the weakness of fallen humankind. Rational emotive behavior therapy adds that the hurts we experience are at least in part due to how we think about what happened. When we tell a grievance story with ourselves as victims, when we consider our experience as utterly unique, we can compound our unhappiness and block forgiveness. So how do we move to forgiveness according to Luskin's view?

Let's look at how the HEAL method works with an imaginary grudge. Let's imagine you are being excluded from positions at work. You have all the qualifications necessary for promotion, but repeatedly people with fewer qualifications are being promoted ahead of you. The first few times this happens you think it may be just bad luck or coincidence, but the evidence mounts that promotion to a position you would like is simply not happening no matter how well you perform, no matter what your qualifications.

How would Luskin's HEAL method apply to this case? The person seeking to forgive begins with the H of HEAL, which stands for *hope*: "I had hoped to participate in these opportunities, to make a contribution, and to feel a sense of being a welcomed and valued member at work." A hope statement includes a goal and an expectation that, in this case, was not realized. Luskin writes, "The E in HEAL stands for Educate. In an E statement we *Educate* ourselves to the possibility of things not turning out the way we would like."[10] So, in our scenario, an E statement would look something like this: "I understand and accept that people sometimes exclude others because they perceive them as less qualified or simply do not like them for personal reasons. Countless other people have gone through what I am going through at work, and much worse." In the E statement, the person seeking to become forgiving acknowledges the reality that hopes are not always realized and that countless people through the ages have experienced the loss of what they wanted.

The A in HEAL stands for *affirming* the positive intention that animated the original hope. In this case, an A statement might take this form: "I commit to making contributions at work insofar as I can. I will participate and receive acceptance insofar as this is available." The L in HEAL stands for a *long-term commitment* to your own well-being. In this case, the person might say something like this: "I will make contributions and welcome acceptance when and where this is possible. I'll look for the opportunities and the friendly people that can be found where I am." Just because some doors were shut for some promotions does not mean that all doors will be shut to every opportunity at this workplace or at some other workplace. Luskin's HEAL method is backed by empirical research and has helped promote forgiveness for countless people, even those suffering catastrophic losses such as the murder of a child.

In their own version of retelling the story, Christians have a theological way of reinterpreting negative experiences. This entails considering things from a "supernatural perspective," trying to see things as God might see them. In this way, we see our story as part of God's story, his providential guidance of all creation. Even negative experiences may be an opportunity for growth because God, somehow, brings good out of our unfortunate situation. As St. Paul says, "We know that all things work for good for those who love God" (Romans 8:28). A classic example of this principle at work is the story told in the book of Genesis of Joseph, whose brothers sold him into slavery in Egypt. As a result of this terrible injustice inflicted on him by his own brothers, Joseph ends up working for Pharaoh. In this position, Joseph is able to save not just himself but also his brothers. When he is reunited with his brothers after so many years, they do not at first recognize him. Joseph says to them, "You meant evil against me; but God meant it for good, to bring it about that many people should be kept alive, as they are today" (Genesis 50:20). Difficult experiences can also bring about an increased awareness of our own weakness and vulnerability, which boost humility and reliance on God. Many saints became saints through their suffering, as did St. Ignatius of Loyola through his battle wounds and St. Augustine of Hippo through his restless heart.

The Christian story is ultimately about God's power to bring good out of evil, to bring healing to the sick, and even life to the dead. Usually we may not understand why God allows bad things to happen to us, but in faith we believe that God's power and love will ultimately right every wrong. Just as Jesus though unjustly and cruelly put to death was gloriously raised, so too every follower of Jesus awaits in faith the ultimate undoing of evil, including all evils personally suffered. Just as Christ's story ends not with Good Friday but Easter Sunday and a reunion with his heavenly Father, so too the story of every Christian ends with the resurrection.

Everett Worthington's book *Forgiving and Reconciling: Bridges to Wholeness and Hope* offers another and perhaps even more powerful way to learn to forgive. As a leading researcher of forgiveness, Worthington knows a lot about forgiveness not just from his decades of distinguished scholarly research in this area, but also because his theories about forgiveness were put to the ultimate test.

On a dark New Year's Eve in 1995, a young man broke into Worthington's seventy-eight-year-old mother's house. When the intruder entered the house, his mother woke up and confronted the man. He struck her with a crowbar; he hit her again and again. As she lay dying, he got a wine bottle and sexually violated her with it. While her lifeblood seeped from her wounds, the killer went through the house and smashed every mirror.

Naturally, when Worthington discovered what had happened to his mother, he was enraged. When he saw his mother's blood on the doors, on the walls, and soaked into the carpet, he was filled with a desire to brutally retaliate against the man who had murdered his mother. Worthington seethed, saying, "I'd like to have him alone in a room with a baseball bat for thirty minutes. I'd beat his brains out."[11]

Worthington could have ruminated endlessly on his mother's death, on his own loss, and on his plans for violent revenge. But he did something else entirely. Soon after the murder, Worthington forgave the man who took his mother's life so brutally. His book *Forgiving and Reconciling* details not just his theory of forgiveness but also how he forgave the man who killed his mom. How did he forgive?

Worthington offers a path that helps people move from unforgiveness to forgiveness, bringing about not just decisional forgiveness but also emotional forgiveness. Worthington's process is captured by the acronym REACH: recall the hurt, empathize with the wrongdoer, altruistic gift of forgiveness, commit to forgive, and hold on to forgiveness.

The R in the REACH process of forgiveness stands for

recall the hurt. What exactly causes the pain? In Worthington's case, the answer is obvious. His hurt is caused by the loss of his mother, by the injustice of the murder, and by the added indignities suffered by his mother as she was dying.

The next and more difficult stage is to *empathize with the wrongdoer.* In this stage, Worthington recommends putting oneself in the offender's shoes and imagining what the offender was thinking, feeling, or experiencing that led to the offending action. St. Thomas Aquinas taught that no agent seeks evil for evil's sake. St. Thomas believed that people choose what they choose because they think what they are choosing is good (i.e., enjoyable, useful, excellent) in some way. Now, they may very well be mistaken, but in choosing what they choose they are seeking something that they *believe* is in at least some respect good. Empathizing with the wrongdoer does not mean that you try to pretend that the wrongdoing was justified or morally right. Empathizing is an effort (and it takes effort) to see the apparent good (however distorted) that the agent was seeking.

In Worthington's case, he imagined what was going through the mind of the person who killed his mother. He imagined a young, impulsive teen who saw what he thought was an empty house. Given that all the lights in the house were turned off and there was no car in the driveway, the teen must have thought no one was home. As he entered the house, an old woman emerged from the bedroom. The teen thought, "Oh no! She's spoiling my perfect crime. She has seen me and will turn me in to the police. If I'm arrested, I'll go to prison for years and years. She will destroy my life! I have to use whatever means I can in order to prevent my life from being ruined." In an impulsive act of fear, anger, and adrenaline, he struck the old woman and then violated her in a drug-induced frenzy. From the young man's perspective in that moment, he was acting in self-defense to preserve his future and avoid going to jail for years.

After empathizing with the wrongdoer, the next stage is the *altruistic gift of forgiveness.* Worthington suggests that we think back on times when we have received this gift from others. In his life, Worthington had needed to be forgiven by others many times, and he always experienced receiving someone's forgiveness as a huge relief, a gift given by the other person. Worthington chose to offer this gift of forgiveness to the criminal who had killed his mother. Rather than choosing revenge, he made the choice to treat the wrongdoer humanely.

The next stage is to *commit to forgive.* We can do this by telling a friend that we have forgiven the offender, by writing a note of forgiveness (not to be given to the offender, but to be kept as a reminder), or by recognizing the forgiveness we've given in some way, such as burning a symbol of our unforgiveness. Worthington committed to forgiveness by writing and speaking about his forgiveness of the man who had killed his mother.

The final stage is to *hold on to forgiveness.* We can forget we've forgiven someone or think that we haven't forgiven just because some negative emotions linger or recur when we see the person we have forgiven. Holding on to forgiveness involves recognizing that feelings may come and go, but the reality is that we have forgiven that person. We might need to remind ourselves that we have forgiven the offender. We might need to reread a letter of forgiveness, look at the charred remains of a symbol of unforgiveness we have burnt, or speak to a friend about the forgiveness we have given. Worthington's book *Forgiving and Reconciling: Bridges to Wholeness and Hope* serves as a tangible reminder of the forgiveness that he gave.

Martin Seligman notes that the REACH method of forgiveness works to increase happiness and reduce the negative fallout of unforgiveness. He writes:

> This all may sound mushy and preachy to you. What transforms it to science is that there are at least eight controlled-outcome studies measuring the consequences of procedures like REACH. . . . Less anger, less stress, more optimism, better reported health, and more forgiveness ensued, and the effects were sizable.[12]

I hope that none of us will ever have to face the catastrophic personal suffering of the murder of a loved one. But virtually all of us could benefit from resolving those smaller yet nagging grievances toward others that we carry in our hearts. If this method works even in the case of murder, surely the REACH method is powerful enough to work on the smaller offenses we have all experienced.

I discovered another helpful way to deal with negative emotions, including but not limited to unforgiveness, in Kelly McGonigal's *The Neuroscience of Change*. When negative emotions threaten to undermine your well-being, McGonigal suggests you write a three-part letter to yourself.[13] First, you detail what you are feeling, not so much the causes of your emotions, but which emotions and the degree to which you are feeling them. Second, you universalize your experience by remembering that the emotions that you are experiencing have been felt by literally billions of other people through the centuries. Nothing is uniquely wrong with you for feeling what you feel. Indeed, experiencing negative emotions is a part of every person's life, a part of being human. Finally, you write yourself advice on handling the situation as if you were a wise, experienced sage. Here's an example of a three-part letter:

Dear [your name here],

I can see why you are upset about what happened when your kids came home from college. Your family reunion turned into a family feud, a symbol of how you are not the parent and spouse that you hoped you would be. You looked forward to an evening of laughter and reconnection, and instead you were confronted with a scene fraught with recriminations and resentment. I can see why you worry about the future of your family. Will this kind of outbreak of hostilities happen every time the whole family gets together? I understand why it made you angry and worried.

But remember that all families bicker from time to time. All kids—especially during their teenage and emerging adult years—frustrate and disappoint their parents. As for spouses bickering, this goes back to a guy named Adam and his wife, Eve.

As a wise, experienced person, I would advise you to

> *remember the big picture. Your family gets along quite well normally, and this incident was an unpleasant aberration from the norm. Remember that you've noted positive improvements in your kids as they move closer to full adulthood. Of course, they are imperfect, as is everyone, but they are also deeply lovable and usually they do get along. Yesterday's unfortunate scene was just that, not the regular course of life, let alone something that will happen forevermore into the future. Keep going. Finish the race you've begun with joy and enthusiasm.*
>
> *Sincerely, Your Wise Advocate*

Writing this kind of letter can help us to deal with negative emotions in such a way that these emotions don't lead to pointless and debilitating ruminations. Writing is a structured activity that externalizes what we experience and helps us to get a better handle on it. Instead of allowing images, memories, and feelings to spin around in your mind, if you write a letter you can at least in part capture the swirl of the emotions and domesticate them. If you write a letter to yourself, a sense of resolution replaces the nagging negativity. Writing letters such as these can help to recapture a sense of balance and equanimity. As the psychologist Robert Emmons points out,

> Research has shown that translating thoughts into concrete language has advantages over just thinking thoughts. We think much faster than we can write or speak. When you put your thoughts into words, either out loud or on paper,

> the thinking process is slowed down. It makes the thoughts more real, more concrete, and helps us to elaborate on them. . . . Putting feelings into words can make a person feel better because doing so dampens activity in the parts of the brain associated with negativity.[14]

Writing such a three-part letter is linked to Luskin's idea of reminding oneself that what one experiences has been experienced by countless people in the past and even now. Indeed, writing such a letter could be a tool to help you reach emotional forgiveness by dispersing negative emotion.

Contemporary psychology can aid us in achieving forgiveness by offering empirically tested techniques and paths that lead us from unforgivenesss, bitterness, and desire for revenge to forgiveness, inner peace, and love for others. The teachings of Jesus about forgiveness are given to heal human relationships, to heal the hurts that we so often carry within ourselves, and to help us to become more like God, who offers his rich mercy to all people.

To forgive others requires inner strength. The same is true for being consistently grateful or for developing a deep spiritual life. The ancient philosophers called these inner strengths "virtues."

| SIX |

The Way of Virtue

For this very reason, make every effort to supplement your faith with virtue, and virtue with knowledge.

2 Peter 1:5, ESV

Being happier is not something that just happens to you. It's not something passive. It's an activity. Christian teaching and positive psychology share these insights.

Thus far in *The Gospel of Happiness*, we've learned about many activities that can increase our happiness, such as praying, expressing gratitude, and forgiving. In order to increase our everyday happiness, we need to do happiness-enhancing activities. Just as medications work to restore health only when taken, in order to become happier, we need to do happiness-boosting activities regularly.[1] They need to become habits.

Aristotle understood habit to be "second nature." We are born with our first nature, but we acquire our second nature through what we do. Habits make us efficient because when we have established a pattern, we expend little mental energy in doing what needs to be done. Our mind likes to make habits, indeed it makes them automatically, so as to free up our attention for more pressing matters or just to be at ease. When we get into our habitual cycle, it can bring us the comfort and pleasure of the familiar. Developing a habit is something like walking through an unmarked forest. The very first time we walk in a particular way through the forest, beating our own trail, the going is tough. But if we walk along the same path each time, and if others join us, the little path eventually becomes a well-trod trail. Habits are understood in positive psychology in terms of neural pathways. Each choice we make shapes our brains to make it more likely that we'll choose the same way again. Our brains seek to be efficient, so as we choose something, it becomes easier to choose that thing again. Each time we choose or decide a particular way, the neural pathways of our mind used for carrying out such a decision become more well trod and easier to walk down again.

When we have a habit, like speaking our native language, the activity is easy, and we experience pleasure in speaking. By contrast, if we do not yet have a habit, the very same activity is burdensome, difficult, and often unpleasant, like speaking a language that you are just beginning to learn.

Both virtues and vices are habits. A virtue is a habit of choosing activities that are conducive to authentic happiness and human flourishing. A vice is a habit of choosing what undermines authentic happiness and human flourishing. Ancient philosophers singled out four habits that are particularly central to a flourishing human life, the four cardinal virtues: practical wisdom, courage, temperance, and justice. Without practical wisdom, we will not know which choices really serve the love of God and neighbor. Without courage, we will fail to love God and neighbor whenever danger of any kind threatens. Without the moderating power of temperance, we will fail in love whenever pleasures tempt us away. And without justice, we will not give to each person what is due to her and thereby fail to love each person. We read in the *Catechism of the Catholic Church* that "the goal of a virtuous life is to become like God."[2] And in becoming like God, we come to share in God's own happiness.[3]

We find a similar emphasis in positive psychology, which focuses on the happiness found in activities giving rise to "flow" and making use of signature strengths. In *Character Strengths and Virtues,* Martin Seligman and Christopher Peterson tackle questions that are relevant to virtuous living such as how to develop character in families, schools, and culture. For in Christian teaching and in positive psychology, becoming happier involves taking action directed toward a challenging goal and requires good interior dispositions, namely strengths.

However, it should be noted that the concept of signature strengths as understood in positive psychology is not identical with older views of virtue as understood by Aristotle and Aquinas.[4] Aristotle thought that virtuous people were rare. Positive psychology teaches that everyone has signature strengths. Aquinas taught that without love, no other true virtue exists.[5] Positive psychology teaches that someone could have signature strengths in some areas, even while lacking the signature strength of love.

Positive psychology supplements the traditional emphasis on character through its empirical orientation, which attempts to in some way measure virtue. Seligman and Peterson describe seven different character strengths that mirror, more or less exactly, the theological and cardinal virtues, namely faith, hope, and love and justice, courage, temperance, and practical wisdom. What is new and significant is that Seligman and Peterson have developed tests that can help people identify their signature strengths. According to their findings, people making use of their signature strengths in new ways not only report greater happiness, but also can shore up, in certain ways, areas of weakness. Finding or creating a link between your own signature strengths and your daily work can greatly augment happiness. Such testing could be used in the Christian community as part of a vocational discernment process. Making use of these tests for determining signature strengths may help you to find a good "fit" between your signature strengths and how you might serve others.

Even if what we are doing is not something that directly makes use of one of our signature strengths, we can often bring our signature strengths to bear on the task at hand. Imagine a bagger at a grocery store who has the signature strength of kindness. In itself, bagging groceries need not have anything to do with kindness. But the clerk could use the occasion of bagging groceries to say something nice—a compliment or a word of encouragement—to each person who is waiting to leave the store. If he chooses to do this, he will likely experience a boost in happiness (not to mention increasing the happiness of others).

Positive psychology can also aid in the development of good habits. Although positive psychology's emphasis on signature strengths appears to be morally neutral (inasmuch as a signature strength could be used for a morally bad as well as for a morally good purpose), the findings of contemporary psychology can aid people to grow in virtue. Positive psychology and contemporary neuroscience have suggested ways in which we can enhance positive habit formation. In his book *The Brain that Changes Itself*, Norman Doidge points out that the plasticity of the brain means that no one is "done," as far as being a fixed and final version of herself. Progress (or regress) occurs daily through the choices we make, by which we shape ourselves, for better or for worse. People of faith, interested in cultivating the habit of doing good acts, can make use of contemporary findings to help themselves to gain or strengthen good habits and break or weaken bad habits.[6]

Forming new habits begins with self-knowledge, particularly awareness of thoughts. As the wise adage goes, "Sow a thought, reap an action; sow an action, reap a habit; sow a habit, reap a character; sow a character, reap a destiny." Good actions giving rise to virtuous habits always begin with good thoughts. Whatever we are unaware of, we cannot choose. Roy Baumeister and John Tierney, in their book *Willpower: Rediscovering the Greatest Human Strength*, suggest that awareness—both self-awareness and awareness of others seeing us—is related to self-control. Daily monitoring of progress (or lack of progress) is key to growth. They write: "Keeping track is more than just knowing where things are. It means knowing where they are in relation to where they should be. . . . Changing personal behavior to meet standards requires willpower, but willpower without self-awareness is as useless as a cannon commanded by a blind man."[7] This insight echoes the advice of spiritual directors who recommend daily examination of conscience to keep track of one's moral growth. St. Ignatius of Loyola, when he was helping people such as the early Jesuits advance in the spiritual life, asked them to be more aware of their thoughts and actions, to take an inventory at least twice a day of how they were doing with a characteristic they were seeking to improve.[8] This practice of the examination of conscience, or Examen, helps us develop a deeper consciousness of what we do and what we fail to do. The first step in habit development, both in breaking bad habits and making good habits, is self-awareness.

Baumeister and Tierney give numerous suggestions about how to build a new habit.[9] First, we should make a resolution to work on one habit at a time, rather than trying to do a total transformation all at once. Trying to quit smoking, lose weight, pray more, and be more patient is likely to end in smoking more, gaining weight, praying less, and having less patience. We are much more likely to achieve success in our resolutions if we dedicate an entire month to one specific resolution—say, reading Scripture slowly and prayerfully for ten minutes a day, rather than attempting multiple resolutions at the same time.

Second, the research suggests that we should write down our specific resolution, review it each morning, and then review how we did each night. If appropriate, we can share our goals with others, such as a spouse, friends, or a spiritual director. A wise spiritual director can help someone understand what is going wrong and can serve as a kind of coach to help a person to advance in love of God and love of neighbor. Robert B. Cialdini found that people are more likely to carry out a resolution if they have made a free, public, and active commitment to the resolution.[10] By telling others, we increase the likelihood that we will develop our new habit. By writing down our resolution, it becomes more "real," and we are more likely to call it to mind at the right moment.

Third, in making resolutions we should draw bright lines

rather than fuzzy lines around the behavior we want to cultivate. A fuzzy line is "I won't overeat." A bright line is "I will eat three healthy meals a day, no more." A fuzzy line is "I won't drink too much." A bright line is "If I drink, I will have three beers or fewer." A fuzzy line is "I won't use the Internet late at night." A bright line is "I will use the Internet only before 9:00 p.m." A fuzzy line is "I will pray sometime each day." A bright line is "I will pray each morning right after breakfast." Bright lines help us to develop good habits because they make it harder to rationalize moving in the wrong direction. We can easily tell whether we've had three beers or fewer. We can more easily rationalize behavior when the lines are fuzzy: "Well, this fifth beer isn't really too much, is it?"

Fourth, effective resolutions are stated positively rather than negatively, even though most resolutions can be put either way. If at all possible, we should strive, in other words, to turn an "I won't" resolution into an "I will" resolution.[11] We more easily pursue a positively stated goal—"I will pray each morning right after breakfast"—than avoid its opposite—"I won't forget to pray." We can more easily identify a path to a positive goal—"I will clean up the kitchen right after dinner to help out"—than chart the innumerable ways to avoid a negative goal—"I won't leave a mess." When the mind has a positive goal, it searches for ways to achieve the goal. The more defined a goal is, the easier it will be for us to identify and narrow down possible strategies for achieving it. When the mind is trying to avoid something, it becomes a bit paranoid in thinking of all the possible ways in which what is to be avoided might show up. By having our goals framed in positive terms, we make it easier to develop the habit we want.

Charles Duhigg, in his book *The Power of Habit: Why We Do What We Do in Life and Business*, also explores contemporary research on how to make a habit and how to break a habit.[12] Christians can put this information to use in building new virtues (good habits) or in breaking old vices (bad habits). In order to understand more about habits, let's begin with breaking a habit.

Let's say I have the habit of drinking excessively. I noticed that going out for a couple beers turns rapidly into losing track of the number of beers I've had. After I've had too much, I say and do things that I regret, and the next morning I feel hungover and cannot work well. Let's say I'm not an alcoholic, but I know that my excessive drinking is undermining love for God and neighbor. I would be a better husband, father, friend, and worker if I cut down on or stopped my habit of drinking too much. How then could I break this habit?

First, in order to break a habit, it helps to study the habit. A hunter is more likely to be successful in killing a mountain lion if he knows all about it—where and when it eats, where it sleeps, the trails it most frequently uses, and so forth. So the first and perhaps most important part of breaking a bad habit is to learn about the habit.

All habits have three basic parts: cue, routine, and reward. What gives rise to the habitual action (what are the cues)? What exactly happens in terms of the routine of carrying out the action (what is the cycle)? What reward does this action bring me (what is the payoff)? Like a three-legged stool, every habit consists of a cue, a routine, and a payoff.

The *cue* prompts the person into action. A cue could be a person. Perhaps every time I go out with one particular friend,

I speak badly about others. A cue could be a time. Every evening I eat too much. A cue could be an emotion. Whenever I get angry, I yell and say things I regret. The cue of a habit consists of the circumstances that give rise to the action. In his *Summa theologiae,* St. Thomas Aquinas listed possible circumstances as follows: "who, what, where, by what aids, why, how, and when."[13] In order to break a habit, we must study the habit carefully to see what gives rise to it in terms of time, place, emotion, situation, persons, events, and other circumstances in which we perform the habitual action. Finding the cues that give rise to the action can help us gain control over the habit. For this reason, the Fourth Lateran Council in 1215 directed that priests make sure that they understand the circumstances of people confessing their sins so as to help them find suitable remedies for improving their lives.[14] When we are more aware of the triggers or cues that prompt us to enter the cycle of behavior, we are more able to alter the course of action. In the case I am imagining, let's say I realize my cue for drinking too much is going out to a restaurant with my friend Frank. I don't drink too much at home or at parties, but I almost always do when I get together with Frank.

Second, what is the *routine* or cycle of the habit? What is the beginning, middle, and end of the cycle? Once prompted by the cue (meeting up with Frank and heading to the restaurant), I rapidly drink the first beer, and I quickly order a second. From then on I go on autopilot and have too much. We walk home from the restaurant, and I stumble into bed. The next morning I can function, but I'm definitely not feeling good, nor am I able to be the best husband, father, and worker. A week or two go by and then the whole process begins again.

The better we understand the routine of a habit, the better able we will be to devise ways of breaking up the routine.

The final factor of habit is the *reward*. What is the payoff for engaging in the routine? Until we consider the habit carefully, it may not be obvious what the payoff for a particular behavior is. In the case of drinking excessively, is it the taste of the beer that I really crave? Do I want to feel the buzz of the alcohol? Do I just *not* want to feel something else? What reward does following this routine deliver or at least promise to deliver? If we can figure out what we are seeking in continuing with the habit, it becomes possible to find other routes to achieving the same goal.

Once we have studied a habit in its three primary dimensions (cue, routine, and reward), we position ourselves to take charge. As we become more aware of the triggers that lead us into the routine, this awareness helps us to move from acting on autopilot (what a habit is all about) to acting in a more deliberate and thoughtful way. If we can recognize the cue for the trigger that it really is, we can then interrupt the thoughtless continuation of the routine. In addition, once we are aware of the triggers that lead us into the routine we wish to avoid, we can pre-plan a new routine.

If I always drink too much alcohol when I go out with Frank, I can pre-plan a course of action with Frank that will limit or even eliminate the routine that is curtailing my happiness. For example, I could bring along only $10 cash when I go out with Frank (who never buys me drinks), and in this way I will limit myself to just one or two drinks. I could arrange for an afternoon walk with Frank rather than head out to a restaurant as we usually do.

When we recognize our cues and know our typical routine, we can experiment with setting up a new reward. If the cool taste of beer is the reward, I could order a nonalcoholic beer like O'Doul's and still have what I crave. Maybe I'd find it easier to limit myself to one or two glasses of wine. Would alternating a beer with drinking a large glass of water make a difference? What if Frank and I took a walk together rather than heading to a restaurant? Perhaps getting a little bit of exercise and a change of scenery would be a better "reward" than consuming alcohol. After experimenting with different rewards, I might discover that what I craved wasn't really the taste of beer, or the buzz of the alcohol, but rather chatting with a friend, which could be done just as well (or perhaps even better) without alcohol. If we experiment, we may be able to find a way to get the "reward" but not undermine our true happiness. We need a new plan.

Probably the most vital part of breaking an old habit is having a plan for an alternative. We do well to say, "I won't do this." We do better to say, "I'll do this other thing instead." Planning what to do in place of the old habit is essential. When the cue arises, although I used to do whatever behavior I'm trying to change, now I'll follow my new plan. For example, many people have given up cigarette smoking by substituting something else, such as chewing on a toothpick, when the urge to smoke hits. The more detailed we can be about what could go wrong to take us off course from our new goal and the more detailed we can be about how we can overcome these obstacles, the more likely we will be to move in the right direction when the cue arises.[15]

Old habits are rarely eliminated entirely, as they can be

reactivated by beginning to do the old actions again. The neural pathways are dormant but still somewhat extant. For this reason, perhaps, people in Alcoholics Anonymous speak of themselves as "recovering alcoholics." Unlike those who have never had the habit of abusing alcohol, these people need to exercise special vigilance to avoid returning to their prior problematic habit.

Setting up a new habit is characteristically somewhat easier than breaking an old habit. Let's say we want to develop the new habit of slowly reading from the Gospels for ten minutes each day to deepen our knowledge and love of Christ and to stimulate love for neighbor. This habit, like all habits, will involve a cue, routine, and reward.

Let's start with the cue. If possible, establish the cue for the new habit in the morning, when your energy and focus are typically higher than later in the day. Time early in the morning is usually less likely to be interrupted than time in the afternoon or evening. The cue could be something that you do every day already—such as getting dressed, eating breakfast, or drinking coffee. Let's say I choose the cue for this new habit to be pouring the morning cup of coffee. What exactly will the routine be? I sit in the comfortable chair where I usually drink my coffee (making the new habit as pleasant as possible) in the light by the window. Each day I slowly read just one scene from the life of Jesus and consider how the Gospel passage applies to me. Notice how the resolution is about a particular time and place and is cast in the present tense. The reward sought is a deeper knowledge and love of God found in a moment of peace, chemically enhanced by the coffee. The potential new habit has its three elements: cue, routine, and reward.

Of course, planning a new habit is relatively easy, but establishing it is harder. Often we start in on a new habit for a few days and then get sidetracked by something as simple as forgetfulness. I might place the Bible on top of the coffeemaker, at least for the first few weeks, in order to remind myself of my new routine. Or perhaps I can set a reminder on a cell phone. Sometimes we will not be able to follow this routine because of travel, early-morning duties, and so forth. A day or two skipped need not derail the establishment of a new habit. These everyday interruptions happen to us all, but we can begin again and continue down the right path. Especially at first it may be hard to be consistent in the new activity, but it becomes easier and easier as time goes on.

Setting up a new habit or breaking an old habit does not happen overnight. Though urban legend holds that we can make a new habit in twenty-one days, in his book *Making Habits, Breaking Habits* Jeremy Dean found that it took on average sixty-six days to create a habit.[16] Can we make a habit even faster? Yes, in some instances, we can. In general, the easier the habit is, the faster one can create the habit. The habit of drinking a glass of water might take just a couple weeks; the habit of running every morning might take months. To create a new habit, we will need patience and willpower. Indeed, both making a new habit and breaking an old habit often require a great deal of willpower. How can we go from weak-willed to strong? Fortunately, contemporary psychology has quite a few tips for developing greater willpower.

| SEVEN |

The Way of Willpower

Oscar Wilde once said, "I can resist anything but temptation." St. Paul concurred when he wrote, "I do not do what I want, but I do what I hate" (Romans 7:15). Whether we call it weakness of will or a lack of self-control, we have all had the experience of *knowing* what is right yet *doing* what is wrong.

When we do wrong, we undermine our own happiness by harming our relationships with God, with other people, and with ourselves. Like many Christians, I've noticed that my self-chosen undermining of loving relationships characteristically arises not from ignorance ("I had no idea that was wrong!") or from malice ("Yeah, this was wrong, but so what!") but from weakness of will ("I knew I shouldn't, but I did it anyway, and now I regret it."). Educated Christians usually *know* the right thing to do (which is great), but even the best-educated Christians sometimes fail to actually *do* the right thing. Weakness of will is not, of course, a uniquely Christian problem. Even the most highly educated among us suffer from doing what they know they shouldn't. For example, although doctors know better than anyone the detrimental effects of obesity, almost half of physicians are overweight.[1]

Much of our unhappiness is self-inflicted. We are all something like the character Patrick Melrose in Edward St. Aubyn's novel *Mother's Milk*. His mistress asks Patrick if he is his own worst enemy. "I certainly hope so," Patrick replies. "I dread to think what would happen if somebody else turned out to be better at it than me."[2] Weakness of will can make us our own worst enemies.

The most important remedy for weakness of will is the grace of God. Indeed, without God's help, no one can become friends with God in this life or in the life to come. Without the help of grace, our natural weakness of will undermines love for God, neighbor, and ourselves. Since grace and nature are two gifts from God that work together, I'd like to focus a bit on some "natural" ways discovered in psychology for strengthening us in times of weakness. Indeed, one way God's grace can be at work in us is by helping us make use of these natural aids in strengthening willpower.

Fortunately, contemporary scientists have discovered remedies that can help anyone struggling with weakness of will. Christians hoping to be more faithful in living out their Christian vocation can learn much from this research. As I mentioned in the introduction, the Second Vatican Council envisioned such uses of psychology to help the faithful mature in the life of faith.[3]

How can scientific research on weakness of will help us to live a better Christian life? Contemporary psychological insights foster advance preparation for success in moments of temptation, combat rationalizations for "giving in" and remedies for the rationalization, and suggest how to handle moments of temptation.[4]

Cartoons depict a person struggling with temptation as having a red devil on one shoulder and a white angel on the other. In his book *The Marshmallow Test: Mastering Self-Control,* the Columbia University psychologist Walter Mischel points out that the human brain does indeed have two systems, a "hot" emotional, impulsive, and quick system and a "cool" reflective, effortful, and calm system.[5] Willpower struggles can be characterized as these two systems coming into conflict. We can achieve greater success in struggles with temptation by empowering the "cool" reasonable aspects of us and by dampening in various ways the "hot" impulsive aspects. Some people think willpower is something you either have or you don't have. But in fact, willpower is something we can develop. It is more like a muscle than like eyesight.

Advance Preparation for Success

Researchers found that we can prepare for success in moments of temptation by strengthening our willpower *before* the occasion arises. Much as lifting weights in training makes an athlete stronger in competition, scientists have established that little acts of self-denial make people stronger in moments of temptation. Small exercises in self-control (e.g., sitting up straight, speaking without slang, not swearing, getting up right away when the alarm goes off, not putting butter on bread) strengthen overall self-control.[6] This insight was discovered centuries earlier by Christian spiritual masters who recommended self-denial and acts of mortification in order for people to advance in the spiritual life.

But too much self-denial can also lead to willpower failure. Just as one can "overtrain" by working out too hard, which leads to injury, so too willpower can be drained. Researchers found that willpower can be drained by such things as making numerous choices and by having to resist a temptation for a long time. For this reason, excessive training of willpower is counterproductive, for overdoing self-denial will not lead to more success in moments of temptation but rather more failure, as our strength will be drained. Exercises in self-denial need not be dramatic or harsh, like fasting on bread and water every day for a year or living on top of a pillar, to have a good effect in strengthening willpower. Much better are small acts of self-denial that exercise but don't exhaust willpower. Eating whatever is least pleasing first at a meal, doing an irksome task promptly and cheerfully, and not putting sugar in our morning cup of coffee are excellent choices. Since we can easily go astray in exercising self-denial (as well as in other matters), we are wise to consult a spiritual director who can help in prudential discernment about what kinds of self-denial would be helpful in our own particular situation.

Timing also matters. If possible, face your struggles to do the right but more difficult thing at the time when you are the strongest. I'm in a mixed marriage. I'm a morning person and my wife is a lifelong night person. My wife wakes up swearing. I go to bed swearing. From seven a.m., while waking the children for school, my wife says she sounds like a prison guard: "If your ass isn't out of that bunk by the time I take my next inhale, I'm going to scale that death trap of a ladder and pull you down by your prepubescent hair!" At least she's colorful. When we get notes home telling us what our kids have said on the blacktop, it's never the standard cursing. In fact, because it's so over the top, the principal always smiles ruefully and says something like: "Well, it's clear he didn't learn *this* at home." And I'm no better at ten-thirty at night, when I'm prone to growling and grumbling like Oscar the Grouch. Maybe when the kids are grown and there isn't a tumbling of bodies fighting for clean underwear and a turn at the sink, my wife and I will become paradigms of calm composure at all hours of the day. I doubt it. In any case, if possible, make the choices you find difficult when you are feeling your strongest.

Although intrinsic rewards for good behavior and the intrinsic punishments for bad behavior motivate best, Jeremy Dean suggests we can also use extrinsic rewards and penalties.[7] In other words, we can strengthen willpower by rewarding ourselves when we choose the good and depriving ourselves when we do not. This way of strengthening willpower is also a part of traditional Christian practice. Doing penance for wrongdoing is a way of motivating ourselves to avoid wrongdoing in the future. Similarly, rewarding ourselves when we choose well can increase the likelihood of making good choices in the future.

Researchers also found that physical exercise is, in the words of Kelly McGonigal, "a willpower miracle." She notes that a five-minute dose of exercise, not an hour-long workout, is often all that is needed to boost willpower.[8] Just a five-minute burst of walking, especially outside looking at green plants, significantly helps restore self-control. It's not bad for your overall physical health either!

I do a lot of homework especially with one of my kids. Although I often enjoy it, it can become a burden for both of us. We start with proving triangles congruent, then translate something Ciceronian from Latin, then look at Puritans in U.S. history. After my long day at work and her long day at school, we can be at each other's throats by the time we take a crack at chemical equations. The solution? A walk around the block in between subjects makes all the difference for us both.

In another interesting finding, Roy Baumeister points to a link between external order and internal strength: "The link between external order and inner self-discipline has been confirmed recently in some remarkable studies."[9] A clean desk may help not only in finding papers, but in boosting self-control. Putting our room in order can help us put our soul in order.

Scientists have also discovered four willpower drainers: sleep deprivation, poor nutrition, alcohol consumption, and stress. If we would like optimal willpower, we need to sleep sufficiently, eat healthily, and drink moderately (if at all). Taking care of these basic bodily needs can substantially increase willpower. As for stress, we cannot simply avoid it entirely, and stress occasions many willpower failures. So what can we do about it?

Unfortunately, some people attempt to relieve stress in ways that do not actually *relieve* them from stress but merely *distract* them from stress. When under stress, some people turn to gambling, shopping, smoking, drinking, eating, playing video games, surfing the Internet, or watching TV for hours. Psychologists have found that these activities are among the *least effective* remedies for stress. Although these activities may distract us from stress, they do not actually alleviate the underlying problem.

What can we do instead? McGonigal notes, "According to the American Psychological Association, the most effective stress-relief strategies are exercising or playing sports, praying or spending time in religious services, reading, listening to music, spending time with friends or family, . . . and spending time with a creative hobby."[10] These activities do not merely *distract* us from stress but actually *relieve* stress. Unfortunately, when we are stressed, we tend to underestimate how much these healthy activities actually relieve stress. Researchers have recommended, therefore, that we make a plan before we're stressed about how to deal with stress. If we wait until the stressful moment, we are more likely to choose ineffective stress relievers precisely because high stress situations impede our most reasonable responses and move us into a panic "fight or flight" mode. When stressed, we think we need to hit sin city—however that is defined for us. Stress propels us to our anesthetizing drug of choice—downing Coronas or lighting up Marlboros or buying at Nordstrom's. Better to make a plan to deal with stress. After working on taxes, I head straight to the gym. When my neighbor yells at me (for no good reason, mind you), I call my friend to vent. When the bills are piling up, I turn on '80s music (okay, this may work for only some people).

One of the most effective ways to avoid lapses in willpower is through what researchers call "pre-commitment." As much as we can, we should arrange our lives so that there is "no way out" for us when we foresee we may have weakness of will. In 1519, the Spanish conquistador Hernán Cortés exercised pre-commitment when he burned his ships so that his men would not be tempted to turn back from the "New World." We can "burn our ships" to make it much more difficult for us to have a willpower lapse. This might mean not going to certain places, not being with certain people, or avoiding particular circumstances that lend themselves to temptation. For more success, we should avoid the near occasion of sin. If possible, we can plan ahead to make it difficult or even impossible to do what we don't want to do.

Finally, it turns out that willpower is contagious and communal. We are much more likely to succeed if we join a group that is struggling with the same willpower challenge. This is part of the success of Alcoholics Anonymous. When often surrounded by others committed to a life of sobriety, people find it easier to choose to live soberly. Research shows that even thinking about about someone with excellent self-control can help strengthen us in moments of weakness. As Walter Mischel points out, "When dealing with temptations, one way to momentarily escape the hot system is to imagine how someone else would behave. It's easier to use the cool system when making . . . choices for others rather than oneself."[11] We can recall saints, living and deceased, who struggled with temptation but did the right thing anyway. To receive social support, we can communicate our struggle with a spiritual director or with a priest in confession. This is also why communal forms of prayer—such as the prayers said at the Mass—

help those struggling to live a Christian life increase their willpower.

Rationalizations and Remedies

Let me now say a word about rationalizations leading to weakness of will and the remedies that can be used to correct these rationalizations. Before a willpower breakdown, people typically say or think to themselves certain things that make giving in to temptation seem justified. For example, people often say, "I know I shouldn't do this, but I'll just do it today, and then tomorrow I will act better." What we needlessly put off until tomorrow most likely will never happen because tomorrow will in all probability be very much like today. It would be better to choose not to give in today, leaving tomorrow an open question, than to give in today and hope that tomorrow will be different. One of the cognitive biases that human beings experience is the illusion that our "future self" of tomorrow will be more disciplined, frugal, and organized, and less stressed than our current self of today. Yet in all likelihood we will be about as disciplined, frugal, organized, and stressed tomorrow as we are today. "Tomorrow" is always tomorrow, and the opportunity to do good is found only in the present of today.

We can ask, "Wouldn't I rather do this tomorrow than today?" McGonigal notes it's better to ask, "Do I really want the bad consequences that come with always putting this off?" Instead of asking, "Do I want this candy bar now?" we can ask ourselves, "Do I want the consequences of eating a candy bar every afternoon for the next year?" When considering a choice, consider what will happen if you choose like this each day. We can always put off what we know we should do until "someday." Today is someday.

Another example of rationalization is that people who have given in to temptation, often say to themselves, "What the hell, I've already [had one drink too many; fill in the blank], so I might as well just totally go for it." Researchers call this the "what the hell" effect. Once someone has done something wrong, the temptation arises to do even more wrong.

The remedy for the "what the hell" rationalization, which gives us permission to give in even more, is self-forgiveness and self-compassion. We need to be kind to ourselves as we would be kind to a good friend who has failed in a particular instance. Aristotle said that the virtuous person is like a friend to himself.[12] Even if we are not yet virtuous, we only acquire virtues if we do what a virtuous person would do. If we are to grow in virtue, we need to be kind, patient, generous, understanding, and compassionate to ourselves as we would be toward a good friend who is suffering and struggling with weakness of will.

Some people think just the opposite. They believe that growth in virtue and better behavior will come about through being harsh, mean, exacting, and tyrannical against themselves. But the psychologists who studied this approach found that it actually led to more willpower failures and worse behavior rather than to fewer failures and better behavior. To be cruel, mean, harsh, and tyrannical with ourselves is also contrary to Christian charity. Jesus calls his followers to a universal love—for all people, excluding no one. But if no one is excluded from the call to love, this means that we should love ourselves. Jesus's command to love our neighbor as ourselves presupposes that we should love ourselves.[13]

If Christians love everyone and forgive all those who harm them, this leads to both decisional self-forgiveness (I choose to treat myself humanely, despite my shortcomings) and emotional self-forgiveness (I let go of the feelings of self-loathing). In some cases, forgiving oneself can be even more difficult than forgiving others. In his book *Moving Forward: Six Steps to Forgiving Yourself and Breaking Free from the Past,* Everett Worthington talks about his struggles to forgive himself.[14] After their mother's murder, the family struggled with grief and trauma, but no one more than Mike Worthington, who was the first person to discover the bloody corpse. In the aftermath, Mike became increasingly depressed and reached out to his psychologist brother, Everett. Although Everett tried to help, Mike eventually committed suicide. Everett felt he did not do what he should have done to prevent yet another tragedy. In fact, he found it much easier to forgive the man who had murdered his mother than to forgive himself for failing to provide adequate help for his brother.

Hold on, you might say. If I forgive myself, I won't ever grow in goodness. I'll stay stuck in lack of love for God and neighbor. If I love myself, I'll end up on the couch, relaxing with a remote control in one hand and a bag of Doritos Cool Ranch chips in the other. Christianity is about the cross of self-denial, not cuddling up in the warm cocoon of self-love and self-forgiveness.

Self-love is not, properly understood, a license for misbehavior, laxity, and self-indulgence. If we love ourselves properly, we will want what is truly best for ourselves, namely to live in harmony with God, other people, and ourselves. If we love ourselves properly, we will choose what is truly good for ourselves as we would for a dear friend in our care or for our child. Self-hatred is sinful because we are called to love all human beings, including ourselves. Self-forgiveness, like forgiving others, does not mean pretending that nothing bad was done, nor does it mean accepting the status quo. Decisional self-forgiveness involves treating yourself humanely as you would treat your best friend. It is good to regret our wrongdoing, but not helpful to say with Woody Allen, "My one regret in life is that I am not someone else." God made each of us, and God made us all worthy of love. Emotional self-forgiveness involves "letting go" of the negative emotions that impede love of self, others, and God. Self-forgiveness leads to more success in moments of temptation.

Sometimes, however, our good actions in the past lead to bad actions in the present. Psychologists call this "moral licensing." Having exercised willpower in a particular matter, particularly if you have been consistently choosing the good, you might say to yourself, "Wow, I am doing so well. I haven't had too many cocktails [or whatever] in a few weeks. I deserve a little reward for all my hard work and success. I think I'll have just a few martinis, since I've been denying myself for so long." Doing good can lead to the rationalization that our wrongdoing isn't really wrong, since after all we deserve to have a reward for our good behavior.

To combat moral licensing, McGonigal suggests we view our actions that display willpower "as evidence that you are committed to your goal."[15] Rather than see a stretch of good behavior as justification for the reward of no longer indulging in good behavior, McGonigal writes, "You need to look at what you have done and conclude that you must really care about your goal, so much so that you want to do even more to reach it."[16] When we frame our successes when our willpower is challenged as evidence of our deep desire to achieve our goals, we are less likely to derail our pursuit of these goals through giving in to a temptation. "Moving beyond the traps of moral licensing," writes McGonigal, "requires knowing that who we are is the self that wants the best for us—and the self that wants to live in line with our core values. When this happens, we will no longer view the impulsive, lazy, or easily tempted self as the 'real' us. We will no longer act like someone who must be bribed, tricked, or forced to pursue our goals, and then rewarded for making any effort at all."[17]

Another rationalization that people use when they are tempted is "I really need this to be happy." "If I give in, this will make me happy," we think to ourselves. Or we might think, "If I can just get enough of it, it will make me happy." Psychologists describe this as the trick of dopamine, a neurotransmitter that induces the feeling that we will be happy if we can just get enough of a particular thing. "When dopamine puts our brains on a reward seeking mission, we become the most risk-taking, impulsive, and out-of-control version of ourselves," McGonigal says. "Importantly, even if the reward never arrives, the promise of reward—combined with a growing sense of anxiety when we think about stopping—is enough to keep us hooked."[18] Dopamine is all about the *promise* of reward, but in following the promptings of dopamine, we often fail to get the actual reward. We get only the promise of happiness but not actual happiness.

The remedy for this rationalization is to honestly ask ourselves the question "Does this really bring true happiness?" The hit off the bong, the bingeing with beer, or the break from our striving after God's highest and best for us might promise us happiness, but does it really deliver? Often dopamine pulls a bait-and-switch tactic, promising reward but actually delivering disappointment. When you give in to temptation, do you really find happiness? Or when you give in, does satisfaction remain elusive?

We have to remember not just the false promises, but the reality that ensues when we give in to temptation. People in recovery from alcoholism speak of "playing the movie to the end." Playing the movie to the end means thinking about not just the "high" they experience briefly from giving in to temptation, but the difficulties and depression that come after the brief enjoyment. The beginning of the movie may seem great, but when we play the movie to the end, we find a conclusion that is unsatisfying, negative, and counterproductive to our ultimate goals.

Handling Moments of Temptation

When we find ourselves in moments of temptation, what should we do? Even if we've prepared well, how can we handle the moment when our will begins to weaken? Contemporary psychology offers some helpful suggestions.

FLEE TEMPTATION

The classic biblical advice "flee from temptation" is justified by empirical research. We can walk, or even run, away from what is leading us where we don't want to go. If possible, create a physical distance between yourself and the temptation. "The good news is, temptation has a narrow window of opportunity. To really overwhelm your prefrontal cortex [the 'cool' part of the brain that helps us to do the harder but right thing], the reward must be available now, and—for maximum effect—you need to see it," McGonigal notes. "As soon as there is any distance between you and the temptation, the power balance shifts back to the brain's system of control."[19] For this reason, Scripture repeatedly admonishes us to flee temptation (1 Timothy 6:9–11). The more distance we create between ourselves and what prompts us to sin, the less likely we will experience a failure in our willpower. As noted earlier, actually physically walking (in this case away from temptation) also strengthens willpower.

REFRAME THE CHOICE

It may be helpful in times of temptation to reframe the choice. McGonigal tells the story of a young medical student who found that checking Facebook was cutting into the time she needed for studying. So when she felt the urge to go on Facebook, she called to mind a simple question: "Is going on Facebook right now worth not becoming a doctor?" She also put a photo of herself in medical garb right by the computer to make more vivid what she would be giving up. When she brought her long-term goals to mind, she found the willpower to continue her studying. Yes, a part of you wants to do what you know you shouldn't do, but a part of you also wants to do the right thing and to be a virtuous person. Willpower can be aided by framing the choice in terms of losing or damaging what you already enjoy—peace of conscience, happiness through friendship with God and neighbor. Generally, people are more reluctant to give up what they already have than to gain what they do not have.[20] People who lose $100 are generally more upset than they are happy at finding $100. As Walter Mischel puts it, "Regardless of age, the core strategy for self-control is to cool the 'now' and heat the 'later'—push the temptation in front of you far away in space and time, and bring the distant consequences closer in your mind." He cites the example of heavy smokers who were able to resist cigarettes when calling to mind long-term consequences like cancer, but gave in immediately when focusing on the enjoyment of smoking.[21] So if we reframe the temptation in terms of losing some good we possess (like positive emotions, engagement, loving relationships, meaning, achievement), we will be less likely to give in to the temptation.

WAIT OUT WHITE BEARS

Just as we have difficulty maintaining an exclusive mental focus as in mindfulness practices, so too we have difficulty excluding what spontaneously comes to mind. Unwanted thoughts, like thoughts about doing something that would undermine love for God or neighbor, come spontaneously to mind. According to legend, the Russian novelist Leo Tolstoy was ordered by his older brother to sit in the corner until he stopped thinking about white bears.[22] Tolstoy found that the more he tried not to think about white bears, the more he continued to think about white bears. Later, psychologists called this the "ironic rebound effect." If we try not to think about white bears (or red licorice or frozen apples or whatever), we will find it nearly impossible not to think about white bears (or red licorice or frozen apples or whatever). Ironic rebound takes place because if we are trying not to think about white bears, we have to continually monitor our thoughts to make sure we are not thinking about white bears. Monitoring our thoughts in this way calls to mind (you got it) white bears. Furthermore, we have a cognitive bias for believing that recurring thoughts reflect the truth. This bias moves us to give in to temptation, since we figure this thought must be true and very important; otherwise why would we think of it so often? In reality, a thought is true if that thought corresponds to reality, even if we have only had that thought once. A thought is false if that thought does not correspond to reality, even if we have that thought regularly. If we are trying to not think about a temptation, we may think about it all the more, and thereby experience more trouble with temptation.

So how can we handle the white bear of ironic rebound? We should give up—give up trying not to think about our temptation. Rather than trying to control the thoughts that pop involuntarily into our minds, rather than seeking to master spontaneously arising inner impulses, we should focus on controlling our actions. No one can control what spontaneously comes to mind. Like the wind that comes and goes where it will, the human mind is distracted with different subjects, images, and memories, often without our deliberate choice. The Harvard Medical School psychiatrist Kevin Majeres compares our situation to that of a bus driver with unruly schoolchildren on the bus. No matter what the passengers (our impulses, thoughts, and memories) call out for us to do, the bus driver still has control of the bus and can reach the destination by focusing on the goal. A wise bus driver does not obey the many (contradictory) voices on the bus, but continues to the goal.[23] We cannot choose which spontaneous thoughts come to mind, so we are not directly responsible for these thoughts. However, whatever thoughts or inclinations come to mind, we can choose and control our actions.

We can also do something else to help with ironic rebound. McGonigal writes: "Studies of brain activation confirm that as soon as you give participants permission to express a thought they were trying to suppress, the thought becomes less primed and less likely to intrude into conscious awareness."[24] We can see here how honesty and openness in spiritual direction can be so helpful for spiritual growth. When we tell another person about our temptations, these temptations become less powerful. St. Ignatius of Loyola noted this truth in his *Spiritual Exercises:* "When the enemy of human nature brings his wiles and persuasions to the just soul, he wants and desires that they be received and kept in secret; but when one reveals them to his good Confessor or to another spiritual person that knows his deceits and evil ends, it is very grievous to him, because he gathers, from his manifest deceits being discovered, that he will not be able to succeed with his wickedness begun."[25] When we are struggling with temptation, confession and spiritual direction are wonderful aids. When a secret temptation is communicated in confidential trust to a spiritual director or confessor, that temptation becomes less powerful.

How can we handle the white bear? We should neither fight it by making efforts not to think about it nor feed it by giving in to temptation. It can be helpful to think abstractly about the temptation. We can ask ourselves, "Just how bad is this temptation on a scale of 1 to 10? How long will the temptation last this time, three minutes, five?" As Walter Mischel notes,

> The effect the stimulus has on us depends on how we represent it mentally. An arousing representation focuses on the motivating, hot qualities of the stimulus—the chewy, sweet quality of the marshmallows or the feel of the inhaled cigarette smoke for the tobacco addict. This hot focus automatically triggers the impulsive reaction: to eat it or smoke it. A cool representation, in contrast, focuses on the more abstract, cognitive, informational aspects of the stimulus (it's round, white, soft, small) and tells you what it is like, without making it more tempting. It allows you to "think cool" about it rather than just grab it.[26]

If we scientifically classify the white bear, we have already engaged the more reasonable part of ourselves and moved away from the more impulsive part. Mischel points out it may help to pretend as if we are observing ourselves as a third party would.[27] This too engages the "cool" system.

We know from long human experience that human feelings

and thoughts of whatever kind do not remain in our minds forever. Even if we *try* to focus on just one thought or just one feeling, our minds in a natural restlessness quickly move to consider other things. Rather than fight the bear by trying not to think about it or feed it by giving in to temptation (when you feed wild animals, they often return with friends), just notice the white bear, realizing that the white bear will soon wander away, and remind yourself of your goal of true happiness through love of God and neighbor.

PRAYER AS A RESPONSE TO TEMPTATION

For this reason, among others, praying in times of temptation is helpful. The grace of God, sought by prayer, strengthens us to be able to do good despite human weakness.[28] When we pray to God to help us in times of temptation, we both notice that we are having the temptation and choose to reinforce our relationship with God rather than damage our relationship with God. When we pray, we remember that we are in the presence of God, who sees us and hears us. This awareness aids willpower because, as the psychologist Roy Baumeister found, when we believe others are looking at us, we have greater self-control.[29] Baumeister also notes that practicing religion helps people to have more self-control in two ways (at least): by "reducing people's inner conflicts among different goals and values" and by developing parts of the brain related to self-control. This can be done through religious practices such as "saying the Rosary, chanting Hebrew psalms."[30] Religion helps reduce inner conflicts by providing clear ultimate priorities. For Christians, Jesus provides an ultimate standard for behavior,

> "Teacher, which commandment in the law is the greatest?" He said to him, "You shall love the Lord, your God, with all your heart, with all your soul, and with all your mind. This is the greatest and the first commandment. The second is like it: You shall love your neighbor as yourself. The whole law and the prophets depend on these two commandments." (Matthew 22:36–40)

Jesus's command that we love God and neighbor provides an ultimate standard by which to resolve conflicts over goals and values. The life of prayer (Rosary, psalms) also helps promote self-control. In focusing on praying, the person repeatedly chooses to continue to pray, despite distractions and temptations to stop. This refocusing and resisting of temptation helps to strengthen a person in other situations as well.

SURF THE URGE

Oscar Wilde once said, "The only way to get rid of temptation is to yield to it."[31] In fact, whatever we do, temptations do *not* last forever. Whether we give in to temptations or do not give in to temptations, all temptations come to an end, normally within ten minutes. Waiting just ten minutes can make a dramatic difference in terms of strengthening willpower. Urges are like waves from the ocean. Like waves, urges come and go. Urges sometimes grow in intensity like a wave getting larger and larger. It may seem as if this "wave" will just keep growing more intense and overwhelming. Some people falsely believe that the only way to reduce an urge is to give in to it. In fact, urges go away whether or not we give in to them. They may grow larger for a while, but they crash on their own like a wave. McGonigal suggests: "Accept those cravings—just don't act on them. When a craving hits, notice it and don't try to immediately distract yourself or argue with it. . . . Surf the urge. When an urge takes hold, stay with the physical sensations and ride them like a wave, neither pushing them away nor acting on them."[32] Faith also calls us not to overestimate the power of temptation as if it were irresistible. In the words of Scripture, "God is faithful and will not let you be tried beyond your strength; but with the trial he will also provide a way out, so that you may be able to bear it" (1 Corinthians 10:13). Commenting on this passage, one early Christian wrote that God "grants us the ability to endure. But it lies with us how we make use of this power given to us, whether vigorously or feebly. There is no doubt that in every temptation we have the power of enduring, provided that we make proper use of the power thus granted."[33] In C. S. Lewis's *Screwtape Letters,* a senior devil advising a junior tempter wrote that "your man has now discovered the dangerous truth that these attacks don't last forever; consequently you cannot use again what is, after all, our best weapon—the belief of ignorant humans, that there is no hope of getting rid of us except by yielding."[34] Oscar Wilde was wrong. Temptations often *seem* irresistible, but in reality they are not. If we wait out a temptation, it will leave of its own accord.

SLOW DOWN YOUR BREATHING

A final strategy for handling moments of temptation recommended by McGonigal is "Breathe your way to self-control."[35] When you slow down your breathing to around four breaths per minute, by exhaling more fully than usual and inhaling more slowly than usual, this prompts a rush of oxygen to the prefrontal cortex, which strengthens the ability to control yourself. This strategy can be combined with prayer. As you slow down your breathing, you could thank God for the many blessings he has given you. As mentioned earlier, St. Ignatius of Loyola practiced prayer using the rhythm of breathing. Praying by breathing, using the body and the mind together, can help a person stand steadfast until moments of temptation subside.

WILLPOWER FAILURE

Given the weakness of human nature, we will all from time to time suffer from failures of willpower. How we handle our failures can be a step toward greater virtue and happiness or toward greater vice and despair. What we should *not* do after we lapse is say to ourselves things like this: "What the hell, I've already had too much to drink. I might as well finish the whole bottle." Or, "I've committed one sin. I might as well commit more sins." When our willpower slips, we can fall into even more failures in an effort to relieve unhealthy guilt and anxiety about the failure. As Archbishop Fulton J. Sheen said,

> When you fail to measure up to your Christian privilege, be not discouraged for discouragement is a form of pride. The

> reason you are sad is because you looked to yourself and not to God; to your failings not to His love. You will shake off your faults more readily when you love God more than when you criticize yourself. God is more lenient than you because he is perfectly good and therefore loves you more. Be bold enough then to believe that God is on your side, even when you forget to be on His.[36]

Following the example and teaching of Jesus, we should extend compassion, forgiveness, and mercy to *all* human beings, including ourselves. We must distinguish therefore between healthy regret (I want to live better and grow from this bad decision) and toxic scrupulosity (I'm a horrible, despicable person whose sin is unforgivable and the worst thing ever). Healthy regret arises from love, because love wants what is good for the beloved, including what is morally good. By contrast, toxic scrupulosity stands in opposition to true love and actually leads to much worse behavior. McGonigal writes,

> If you think that the key to greater willpower is being harder on yourself, you are not alone. But you are wrong. Study after study shows that self-criticism is consistently associated with less motivation and worse self-control. It is also one of the single biggest predictors of depression, which drains both "I will" power and "I want" power. In contrast, self-compassion—being supportive and kind to yourself, especially in the face of stress and failure—is associated with more motivation and better self-control.[37]

When we fail, McGonigal points out that these failures are great opportunities to learn how to succeed in the future. We can improve our self-control by seeing how and why we lose control. We should look for patterns of behavior: the who, what, where, why, how, and when of our lapses. When we find patterns in our unwanted behavior, we can then prepare to navigate through the situation better in the future.

Since everyone experiences failures of willpower, everyone has—to a greater or lesser degree—a sense of guilt, a sense of failure to be who they should be. Psychology cannot take away our guilt. Psychology may be able to diminish or even get rid of feelings of guilt, but the fault that gave rise to the feelings remains.[38] A dentist can give someone Novocain so that the infected tooth doesn't cause pain, but the infection, and the danger that the infection poses to the health of the person, remains. So, too, negative feelings prompted by guilt over wrongdoing may be eliminated, but the separation from God and neighbor created by the wrongdoing remains.

But, someone might say, wouldn't it be enough simply to eliminate the feelings of guilt? In fact, eliminating feelings of guilt while not addressing the guilt that gives rise to the feelings may make the situation worse. Guilt, as Aaron Kheriaty points out in his book *The Catholic Guide to Depression*, is a bit like physical pain.[39] When people are healthy, pain warns them that something has gone wrong. It might seem that to eliminate all pain would be a great benefit to humankind. And there are people who are incapable of experiencing pain. They have chronic insensitivity to pain syndrome (CIPS). For these people, cutting off their fingers causes no more pain than trimming the fingernails of a normal person. But people with CIPS characteristically do not live to adulthood because as children they die of injuries that they did not even realize they had. Such people often scratch their eyes with such force that they become blind. They pull out their own teeth, not realizing the harm involved. In a similar way, someone who is overly sensitive to pain also suffers a disability. A person who feels the slightest pinprick as if it were a gunshot wound is disabled from engaging in a full life. Pain, in the right amount and for the right reasons, is necessary for a healthy life, because pain indicates that there is some threat or injury to the health of the body.

In a similar way, feelings of guilt over wrongdoing are necessary for spiritual health. Like pain, feelings of guilt can motivate us to act to promote our spiritual health. Like pain, the ability to feel guilt can be deficient or excessive. The psychopath is a person deficient in feelings of guilt—he kills in cold blood and feels no remorse. To a lesser degree, people who are insensitive in conscience harm their neighbor and neglect the love of God but experience no feelings of guilt. On the other extreme, someone suffering from scrupulosity suffers feelings of exaggerated guilt at the smallest perceived fault. "I'm so horrible; I cut short my time of prayer three minutes early! I'm going straight to hell!" Both insensitivity of conscience and scrupulosity harm our spiritual health because in different ways they each undermine love of God and love of neighbor.

The Gospel is called the "Good News" because God in Christ frees us from our failures. God wants to free us both from feelings of guilt and from guilt itself. Yes, we fail, but God does not leave us wallowing in our failures but loves us even in our failures. This gift of release from our failures, both in terms of forgiveness and in terms of the knowledge that God always loves us even as we fail, brings deep gratitude. Forgiveness also reduces one of the primary causes of failure—negative feelings. In this, as is so many matters, Christianity is not the enemy of psychological health but its friend.

Helping Others Boost Their Willpower

The most obvious way of helping other people whose willpower is being tested is by practicing good behavior ourselves. Personal example is powerfully infectious, and we should not underestimate the power our own choices have on all the people with whom we have contact as well as those people's friends, family, and acquaintances. Human beings, as social animals, influence one another both consciously and unconsciously. If someone we know gains weight, quits smoking, or begins to pray more, we are much more likely to gain weight, quit smoking, or pray more. So if we develop better willpower, we will help all those with whom we have contact (as well as their friends and family) to develop better willpower. We have direct power of free choice only over ourselves, but we have indirect influence over countless people. Just as the flu is spread from person to person, so too increases in willpower can be spread from person to person.

Parents, teachers, and pastors can also help those in their care to have better willpower through the way that they interact with them. As Walter Mischel points out, "Give nine-year-old children compliments (for example, on their drawings), and they will choose delayed rather than immediate rewards much more often than when given negative feedback on their work. And what holds for children applies to adults. In short, we are less likely to delay gratification when we feel sad or bad."[40] When we are kind to others and compliment what is genuinely good in them, we are helping others to be their best selves.

A study at Stanford University looked at the way in which appeal using verbs like "Voting is a civic duty" and appeal using nouns as in "Voters do their civic duty" led to different outcomes of persuasion. When speakers use nouns ("voters," rather than "voting"), they make an appeal to roles and identity, and people are more likely to vote when their identity as a voter is at stake than when an appeal is made using verbs.[41] In motivating behavior, nouns are more powerful than verbs. The same effect was found with using the word "cheating" versus the word "cheaters." When appeal was made to nouns of identity, as in "Cheaters ruin the validity of the study," fewer people cheated than when verbs were used when subjects were told, "Cheating ruins the validity of our study." Christian moral teaching—in churches, classrooms, and conversations—may have increased effectiveness when appeal is made to nouns that designate identity rather than verbs that set forth rules.

In *Made to Stick: Why Some Ideas Survive and Others Die*, Chip and Dan Heath note that an appeal to identity proved more effective than an appeal to consequences in motivating people to stop littering.[42] Providing statistics about how much litter damages the environment, or how much it costs taxpayers to clean up the mess, didn't do much to reduce littering. What did work was an appeal to a stereotypical macho Texan who "doesn't mess with Texas" by littering. People can be motivated by an appeal to an identity that people want to have or even an identity that people do not want to have. Kelly McGonigal notes:

> An intervention at Stanford University took a very different approach to reducing a behavior among undergraduate students. Researchers designed two different flyers to discourage binge drinking. One took a rational approach listing scary statistics about drinking like, "One night of heavy drinking can impair your ability to think abstractly for thirty days." . . . The other flyer linked drinking with the social lepers of university life: graduate students. This flyer showed a graduate student drinking, along with the warning, "Lots of graduate students at Stanford drink . . . and lots of them are sketchy. So think when you drink. Nobody wants to be mistaken for this guy."[43]

The flyers taking the rational, consequences-based approach were put in one residence hall. The flyers taking the identity approach were put in another. After two weeks, students in the dormitory with the identity approach flyers reported 50 percent less drinking than students in the dormitory with the consequences approach flyers. There are groups we want to join and other groups with which we would never want to identify.

Christians have a rich vocabulary for speaking about ethics in terms of identity and models of behavior. We speak of what "good Christians do," we speak of the Good Samaritan, and we speak of the saints. We speak of Christian disciples, followers of Jesus, and the humble and contrite of heart. The more we speak about the way to live in terms of identity, the more motivating our speech is likely to be. In doing so, we follow the example of Jesus, who in his parables gives us models with which to identify and models with whom we do not want to identify—Lazarus and the rich man (Luke 16:19–31), the tax collector and the Pharisee (Luke 18:9–14), the persistent widow and the unjust judge (Luke 18:1–8).

While Christians can help one another by speaking about the ethical life in terms of identity, we can also inadvertently make living an ethical life more difficult by emphasizing how many people are not living a Christian life. Parents, teachers, and preachers who emphasize the doom and gloom of misbehavior may inadvertently prompt even more misbehavior. People are strongly influenced by what psychologists call "social proof." The belief that many or even most people are doing something powerfully influences other people to do the same thing. Advertisers have used this "bandwagon effect" to sell products for years. So to emphasize that many or most people are doing something bad may actually lead more people to do the same. In their book *Yes!: 50 Scientifically Proven Ways to Be Persuasive*, Noah Goldstein, Steven J. Martin, and Robert Cialdini note that people are strongly influenced by social proof, even when the example is negative. Researchers set up an experiment in Arizona's Petrified Forest National Park in which the sign read, "Many past visitors have removed the petrified wood from the park, changing the natural state of the Petrified Forest." The sign was accompanied by a picture of a number of park visitors taking wood. Goldstein, Martin, and Cialdini write, "In a finding that should petrify the National Park's management, compared with a no-sign control condition in which 2.92 percent of pieces were stolen, the social proof message resulted in *more* theft (7.92 percent). In essence, it almost tripled theft. Thus, theirs was not a crime prevention strategy; it was a crime *promotion* strategy."[44] We are deeply influenced by what we think others are doing. This is true particularly of young people and particularly in times of uncertainty.

Knowledge of the power of social proof should provide a caution for preachers, teachers, and parents who emphasize how many people do this or that behavior contrary to Christian teaching. Much better would be to use social proof as a way of motivating the kinds of behaviors that we want to encourage. For example, about 40 percent of Americans, 118 million people, report that they attend church services each week.[45] This is more people than watch the Super Bowl (111.5 million).[46] Many more people report they attend at least monthly, and more than 60 percent of Americans say they plan to attend church on Easter.[47] More than half (55 percent) of Americans pray every day.[48] Three out of four call themselves Christians. These facts normalize (and influence) people to practice similar behaviors. Finding and emphasizing good news can, by the power of social proof, powerfully motivate others to create even more good news.

I'd like to offer a final suggestion on persuasion, especially for parents. In the famous Milgram experiment at Yale University measuring obedience, an authority figure instructs the research participant to give electric shocks to another person (the student) in increasing intensity. The study found that when ordered by an authority figure, 65 percent of participants delivered the maximum voltage to the student, even though the student was crying out and mentioning a heart problem.[49] The study also found that the physical distance between the authority figure and the participant made a difference to obedience. The closer the authority figure was physically to the participant the more likely obedience became.

The practical import of this finding for parents is huge. You can yell from across the room to your son or daughter, "Can you unload the dishes, please." But children are much more likely to obey if you get up and move right next to *them* and then ask them to put away the clean dishes. What parent would not like less fighting and disobedience and more prompt compliance? By moving into physical proximity to their children, parents can increase the likelihood of children obeying without parents raising their voices, engaging in extended debate, or threatening punishments.

Willpower Is Not Enough

Willpower is something that we all need in order to live a flourishing life. Fortunately, contemporary research into willpower provides numerous ways to strengthen our willpower and to find success even in times of temptation. But human willpower is always insufficient for the happiness we crave. For this, we need grace. The Christian teaching on the necessity of God's grace for acting well reinforces humility and enhances compassion. When humble Christians see someone failing spectacularly in the moral life (say, a high school teacher arrested for driving under the influence of heroin after robbing a 7-Eleven for Twinkies), they often say, "There, but for the grace of God, go I." The phrase is also a powerful reminder that our willpower is not sufficient to get us where we want to go—our heavenly home. Indeed, without grace, our willpower is not enough even to make us morally good in a human sense. In fact, we need God's grace to choose the natural remedies mentioned in this chapter. It is the unearned gift of God's abundant grace through Christ that makes the Gospel such good news.[50]

CONCLUSION

In this book, I have explored the intersection of psychology, especially positive psychology, and Christian spirituality and practice. Certainly some forms of psychology are inconsistent with Christianity, as Paul Vitz pointed out in *Psychology as Religion: The Cult of Self-Worship.*[1] Freud's atheistic materialism, and reduction of theism to a childish desire for a father figure as a savior from helplessness, exemplifies this conflict. Yet the full history of psychology and Christian belief is more complicated and interesting. For example, in his recent book *Psychology and Catholicism: Contested Boundaries*, Robert Kugelmann addresses the ways in which psychology and Catholicism have, in various ways, collaborated, commingled, and, only at times, contradicted each other.[2] The time period highlighted in this fascinating study ends in the mid-1960s, before the advent of what is called "positive psychology." This contemporary development in the study of behavior and mental processes opens the door to new ways of conceiving the relationship of psychology to Christianity. Traditionally, psychology has focused on pathologies, such as bipolar disorder, anxiety, and depression. In 1998, Martin Seligman dedicated his term as president of the American Psychological Association to the study of the positive: optimism rather than helplessness, signature strengths rather than pathology, and growth in happiness rather than depression. Far from finding psychology to be an enemy of the Christian faith, many of the studies of positive psychology point to the wisdom of Christian practices, such as prayer, forgiveness, and gratitude, for a flourishing life. I have also noted that in many ways the findings of positive psychology can aid a Christian in living a Christian life by suggesting new empirically tested ways to practice forgiveness and gratitude, by providing empirically tested ways to increase happiness by forgiving those who have trespassed against us, by exploring the power of prayer, and by helping to strengthen willpower.

The explosion of research and new findings in the field of psychology finds an echo in the thirteenth century. At that time Christians had rediscovered the writings of Aristotle, and his philosophy caused a sensation. Some Christians feared these writings, seeing in them various contradictions between what Aristotle taught and what Christian revelation taught. For instance, Aristotle seemed to teach that the world was eternal, that there was just one soul shared by everyone, and that God's Providence did not extend to lowly, earthly things. Other Christians embraced the teachings both of Aristotle and of Christian revelation, even though these views were acknowledged as contradictory. St. Thomas Aquinas, following his teacher St. Albert the Great, proposed another, and to my mind better, way to deal with the new teaching of Aristotle. St. Thomas held that ultimately faith and reason must be compatible because the truths of faith are revealed by God and the truths of reason arise from God's created order. God does not contradict himself, so the truths of the Book of Grace (God's Revelation) and the Book of Nature (truths known by reasoning about God's creation) are compatible. For this reason, Aquinas undertook an intensive study of Aristotle. St. Thomas began this study when he was a student with Albert and continued until Aquinas stopped writing just before his death. His study enabled him to bring about a powerful new synthesis of the best of Augustinian theology and Aristotelian insight.

I believe Christian teaching now stands in a similar relationship to psychology. In this book, I have sought to show several things. First, many of the empirically verifiable findings of positive psychology show the wisdom of the Christian tradition. Just as Aristotelian metaphysics provided a new basis for the natural theology of Aquinas's time, so too, positive psychology provides a basis for a natural moral theology in our own time. Christian warnings about the dangers of greed, coveting a neighbor's goods (social comparison), and pride find an empirical verification in positive psychology. Likewise, positive psychology vindicates the wisdom of Christian teaching on the importance of forgiveness, of gratitude, of humility, and of serving one's neighbor. The philosopher Friedrich Nietzsche thought that the practice of Christianity would drain the love, life, and happiness from people.[3] The findings of positive psychology show, by contrast, that traditional religious practice can contribute to all aspects of flourishing as understood in positive psychology: positive emotion, engagement, relationships, meaning, and achievement. Positive psychology also can be a service to Christian believers by helping them in their struggles with willpower, by providing new motivations for prayer, and by helping them identify their signature strengths.

Are there ways that positive psychology contradicts Christian belief? Indeed, there are certainly numerous instances where positive psychologists contradict Christian teaching. For example, Martin Seligman is skeptical of God's existence,[4] Jonathan Haidt believes that "good" and "evil" are merely subjective matters of perspective,[5] and Ed Diener and Robert Biswas-Diener define "happiness" in purely subjective terms.[6] The list could be extended.

However, these views are not the empirical findings of positive psychology but rather the personal philosophical views of these psychologists. In my reading of positive psychology, I have not found a single empirical finding or any recommendation for increasing happiness that contradicts Christian teaching. At times, positive psychologists do engage in philosophical or even theological speculation, some of which is problematic. Nevertheless, for the most part, positive psychologists steer clear of philosophical and theological matters, which are beyond their professional training and expertise.

The world is of such complexity that specialization is necessary to achieve deep understanding. You wouldn't go to your pastor when questions arise about medical issues or tax rates (unless, of course, your pastor happens also to be a physician or a CPA). When we have questions about our physical health or our tax situation, we are wise to seek out a physician or tax attorney. Similarly, psychologists are not reliable guides when theological or philosophical questions arise, since their training and expertise are not in these areas.

Of course, the relationship between psychology and theology is much more complicated (and interesting) than what I have sought to describe in this book.[7] But my goals have been more modest. I hoped to write a book that would be helpful for Christians by providing a glimpse into an exciting new development called positive psychology which can significantly enrich their lives and provide surprising new justifications for practices recommended by Jesus himself. *The Gospel of Happiness* is good news indeed.

| NOTES |

INTRODUCTION

1. St. Augustine of Hippo, *On Christian Doctrine,* Augustine. Nicene and Post-Nicene Fathers (Grand Rapids, MI: Eerdmans, 1984), II.18.

2. St. Thomas Aquinas, *Summa theologiae* I-II, 109, 1, ad 1.

3. Mary K. O'Neil and Salman Aktar, eds., *On Freud's "The Future of an Illusion"* (London: Karnac Books, 2009), p. x.

4. Richard Webster, *Why Freud Was Wrong: Sin, Science, and Psychoanalysis* (New York: Basic Books, 1995); Frederick Crews, ed. *Unauthorized Freud: Doubters Confront a Legend* (New York: Penguin Books, 1999).

5. Pope Francis, *Evangelii Gaudium* 1. See also Pope St. John Paul II, *Veritatis Splendor* 9; St. Thomas Aquinas, *Summa theologiae* I-II, q. 3; St. Augustine of Hippo, *On the Morals of the Catholic Church.*

CHAPTER 1 The Ways to Happiness

1. Martin Seligman, *Flourish: A Visionary New Understanding of Happiness and Well-Being* (New York: Simon and Schuster, 2011), chap. 1.

2. Ed Diener and Robert Biswas-Diener, *Happiness: Unlocking the Mysteries of Psychological Wealth* (Malden, MA: Blackwell, 2008), p. 4.

3. David G. Myers, *The Pursuit of Happiness: Discovering the Pathway to Fulfillment, Well-Being, and Enduring Personal Joy* (New York: William Morrow, 1993), p. 183.

4. Ibid.

5. Aaron Kheriaty, with Fr. John Cihak, *The Catholic Guide to Depression: How the Saints, the Sacraments, and Psychiatry Can Help You Break Its Grip and Find Happiness Again* (Manchester, NH: Sophia Institute Press, 2012), pp. 36–37.

6. Phyllis Zagano and C. Kevin Gillespie, "Ignatian Spirituality and Positive Psychology," *The Way* 45, no. 4 (October 2006): 50.

7. Kelly McGonigal, "What the Hell: How Feeling Bad Leads to Giving In," chap. 6 in McGonigal, *The Willpower Instinct: How Self-Control Works, Why It Matters, and What You Can Do to Get More of It* (New York: Penguin Books, 2012).

8. Barbara Fredrickson, *Positivity: Top-Notch Research Reveals the 3 to 1 Ratio That Will Change Your Life* (New York: Three Rivers Press, 2009).

9. Gretchen Rubin, *The Happiness Project: Or, Why I Spent a Year Trying to Sing in the Morning, Clean My Closets, Fight Right, Read Aristotle, and Generally Have More Fun* (New York: Harper-Collins, 2009), p. 215.

10. E. Hatfield, J. T. Cacioppo, and R. L. Rapson, "Emotional Contagion," *Current Directions in Psychological Science* 2, no. 3 (1993): 96–99.

11. Sonja Lyubomirsky, *The How of Happiness: A Scientific Approach to Getting the Life You Want* (New York: Penguin Books, 2007), p. 265.

12. Barbara Fredrickson, *Love 2.0: How Our Supreme Emotion Affects Everything We Feel, Think, Do, and Become* (New York: Hudson Street Press, 2013), p. 82.

13. St. Ignatius of Loyola, *Spiritual Exercises*, Fifth Rule.

14. Mihaly Csikszentmihalyi, *Flow: The Psychology of Optimal Experience (*New York: HarperPerennial, 1990).

15. Leo Tolstoy, *Anna Karenina* (New York: Penguin Classics, 2000), pp. 252–53.

16. An excellent exploration of the meaning of vocation is found in Germain Grisez and Russell Shaw, *Personal Vocation: God Calls Everyone by Name* (Huntington, IN: Our Sunday Visitor, 2003).

17. Seligman, *Flourish*, p. 21.

18. Scott Stossel, "What Makes Us Happy, Revisited," *Atlantic Monthly*, April 24, 2013, http://www.theatlantic.com/magazine/archive/2013/05/thanks-mom/309287/.

19. Lyubomirsky, *How of Happiness*, p. 250.

20. Ibid.

21. Grisez and Shaw, *Personal Vocation*.

22. For more on marital love, see Christopher Kaczor and Jennifer Kaczor, *The Seven Big Myths About Marriage: What Science, Faith, and Philosophy Teach Us About Love and Happiness* (San Francisco: Ignatius Press, 2014).

23. Seligman, *Flourish*, p. 17.

24. William Lane Craig, "Does God Exist?" Reasonable Faith, http://www.reasonablefaith.org/does-god-exist-1.

25. Seligman, *Flourish*, p. 21.

26. http://www.latimes.com/entertainment/movies/la-et-mn-robin-williams-last-days-20140813-story.html#page=1.

27. Tal Ben-Shahar, *The Pursuit of Perfect: How to Stop Chasing Perfection and Live a Richer, Happier Life* (New York: McGraw-Hill, 2009), p. 3.

28. Sonja Lyubomirsky, *The Myths About Happiness: What Should Make You Happy, but Doesn't, What Shouldn't Make You Happy, but Does* (New York: Penguin Press, 2013), p. 120.

29. Tal Ben-Shahar, *Happier: Learn the Secrets to Daily Joy and Lasting Fulfillment* (New York: McGraw-Hill, 2007), p. 25.

30. Fredrickson, *Love 2.0*, p. 140.

31. Cited in Michael Alex McDonald, *God Is More Than a Good Idea* (Bloomington, IN: Xlibris, Corp., 2011) p. 25.

32. Eleonore Stump, *Wandering in Darkness: Narrative and the Problem of Suffering* (Oxford: Oxford University Press, 2012).

33. Fulton J. Sheen, *The Quotable Sheen: A Topical Compilation of the Wit, Wisdom, and Satire of Archbishop Fulton J. Sheen* (New York: Doubleday, 1989), p. 134.

34. As quoted by Peter J. Kreeft, *Catholic Christianity: A Complete Catechism of Catholic Beliefs Based on the Catechism of the Catholic Church* (San Francisco: Ignatius Press, 2001), p. 117.

35. See Kheriaty, *Catholic Guide to Depression*, pp. 162–66.

36. St. Thomas Aquinas, *Summa contra Gentiles* 1.4–5.

37. *Gaudium et Spes* 22: *Acta Apostolicae Sedis* 58 (1966), 1042–43; Pope St. John Paul II, *Redemptor Hominis* (encyclical, March 4, 1979), 10.

38. Cited in Bruce Tuckman and David Monetti, *Educational Psychology* (Belmont, CA: Cengage Learning, 2011), p. 560.

39. Lyubomirsky, *How of Happiness*, p. 20.

40. On this topic, see Kheriaty, *Catholic Guide to Depression*.

CHAPTER 2 **The Way of Faith, Hope, and Love**

1. For more on the theological virtues, see Christopher Kaczor, *Thomas Aquinas on Faith, Hope, and Love* (Naples, FL: Sapientia Press of Ave Maria University, 2008).

2. Martin Seligman, *Authentic Happiness: Using the New Positive Psychology to Realize Your Potential for Lasting Fulfillment* (New York: Simon and Schuster, 2002), p. 59.

3. Miguel Farias, Anna-Kaisa Newheiser, Guy Kahane, and Zoe de Toledo, "Scientific Faith: Belief in Science Increases in the Face of Stress and Existential Anxiety," *Journal of Experimental Social Psychology* 49, no. 6 (2013): 1210–13.

4. A. C. Kay, J. A. Whitson, D. Gaucher, and A. D. Galinsky, "Compensatory Control: Achieving Order Through the Mind, Our Institutions, and the Heavens," *Current Directions in Psychological Science* 18, no. 5 (2009): 264–68.

5. M. Inzlicht, A. M. Tullett, and M. Good, "The Need to Believe: A Neuroscience Account of Religion as a Motivated Process," *Religion, Brain and Behavior* 1, no. 3 (2011): 192–212; A. Norenzayan and I. G. Hansen, "Belief in Supernatural Agents in the Face of Death," *Personality and Social Psychology Bulletin* 32, no. 2 (2006): 174–87.

6. G. G. Ano and E. B. Vasconcelles, "Religious Coping and Psychological Adjustment to Stress: A Meta-analysis," *Journal of Clinical Psychology* 61, no. 4 (2005): 461–80.

7. Jonathan Haidt, *The Happiness Hypothesis: Finding Modern Truth in Ancient Wisdom* (New York: Basic Books, 2006), p. 195.

8. See David Scott, *The Love That Made Mother Teresa: How Her Secret Visions and Dark Nights Can Help You Conquer the Slums in Your Heart* (Manchester, NH: Sophia Insitute Press, 2013).

9. Ephesians 2:8; *Catechism of the Catholic Church* 1216; St. Thomas Aquinas, *Summa theologiae* III, q. 66, a. 11.

10. Cited in Randy Boyagoda, "Cordially, Richard John Neuhaus," *First Things* (August 2012): 18.

11. Alexander Pruss, "Loss of Faith," *Alexander Pruss's Blog,* April 6, 2009, http://alexanderpruss.blogspot.com/2009/04/loss-of-faith.html.

12. Joseph Ratzinger, *Introduction to Christianity* (New York: Herder and Herder, 1970), p. 17.

13. Ibid., p. 18.

14. Christopher Peterson and Martin Seligman, *Character Strengths and Virtues: A Handbook and Classification* (New York: Oxford University Press, 2004), chap. 27.

15. Scott, *Love That Made Mother Teresa*, p. 57.

16. See Sonja Lyubomirsky, *The How of Happiness: A Scientific Approach to Getting the Life You Want* (New York: Penguin Books, 2007), p. 208. For a philosophical account of the distinction, see Alasdair MacIntyre on goods external and internal to practices in *After Virtue*, 3rd ed. (Notre Dame, IN: University of Notre Dame Press, 2007), chap. 14.

17. *Catechism of the Catholic Church* 1817.

18. Jerry Walls, *Hell: The Logic of Damnation* (Notre Dame, IN: University of Notre Dame Press, 1992); Michael Murray, "Heaven and Hell," chap. 12 in Murray, ed., *Reason for the Hope Within* (Grand Rapids, MI: Eerdmans, 1999).

19. See *Catechism of the Catholic Church* 1472.

20. St. Augustine of Hippo, vol. 35 of *Against Julian, The Fathers of the Church* (Washington, DC: The Catholic University of America, 2010), p. 254.

21. Bishop Fulton Sheen put the point as follows, "Heaven is very close to us because heaven is related to a good life in much the same way that an acorn is related to an oak. An acorn is bound to become an oak. He who does not have heaven in his heart now will never go to heaven, and he who has hell in his heart when he dies will go to hell. We must not think that heaven is related to a good life in the same way a gold medal is related to study. Because a gold medal need not follow study. It is purely extrinsic to study. Rather, heaven is related to a good and virtuous life in just the same way that knowledge is related to study. One necessarily follows the other. Hell is not related to an evil life in the same way that spanking is related to an act of disobedience. Spanking need not follow an act of disobedience. As a matter of fact, it rarely follows disobedience today. Rather, it is related in the same way that corruption is related to death. One necessarily follows the other. Therefore, heaven is not just a long way off, we

are not to postpone it. It is here. That is to say, it begins here." Fulton J. Sheen, *Through the Year with Fulton Sheen: Inspirational Readings for Each Day of the Year* (San Francisco: Ignatius Press, 2003), pp. 221–22.

22. Cited in Regis Martin, *The Last Things: Death, Judgment, Hell, Heaven* (San Francisco: Ignatius Press, 1998), p. 39.

23. Sheen, *Through the Year with Fulton Sheen*, p. 220.

24. C. S. Lewis, *The Great Divorce: A Dream* (New York: HarperCollins, 1973), p. ix.

25. Ibid., p. 69.

26. Woody Allen, *Four Films:* Annie Hall, Manhattan, Interiors, Stardust Memories (New York: Random House, 1982), p. 4.

27. Viktor Frankl, *Man's Search for Meaning* (Boston: Beacon Press, 1984), p. 84.

28. Martin Seligman, *Learned Optimism: How to Change Your Mind and Your Life* (New York: Vintage, 2006).

29. Walter J. Ciszek, *He Leadeth Me* (San Francisco: Ignatius Press, 1995), p. 12.

30. St. Paul wrote perhaps the most famous and beautiful praise of love: "If I speak in the tongues of men or of angels, but do not have love, I am only a resounding gong or a clanging cymbal. If I have the gift of prophecy and can fathom all mysteries and all knowledge, and if I have a faith that can move mountains, but do not have love, I am nothing. If I give all I possess to the poor and give over my body to hardship that I may boast, but do not have love, I gain nothing. . . . Love never fails. But where there are prophecies, they will cease; where there are tongues, they will be stilled; where there is knowledge, it will pass away. For we know in part and we prophesy in part, but when completeness comes, what is in part disappears. When I was a child, I talked like a child, I thought like a child, I reasoned like a child. When I became a man, I put the ways of childhood behind me. For now we see only a reflection as in a mirror; then we shall see face to face. Now I know in part; then I shall know fully, even as I am

fully known. And now these three remain: faith, hope and love. But the greatest of these is love" (1 Corinthians 13:1–13).

31. Alexander Pruss, *One Body: An Essay in Christian Sexual Ethics* (Notre Dame, IN: University of Notre Dame, 2013), chap. 2. We can, further, distinguish the act of love, the habit of love, and the emotion of love. Acts of love reflect and are motivated by goodwill, appreciation, and appropriate seeking of unity. The habit of love remains in each person even when acts of love are absent. In virtue of our habit of speaking English, we are English speakers, even when sleeping. So too, a loving father still loves his children when he is sleeping, even though he is not doing acts of love for them while sleeping. Finally, love can also be considered an emotion, an emotion that draws and characteristically arises within the one who loves, encouraging them to acts of goodwill, appreciation, and unity. For an interesting exploration of love as an emotion from an empirical perspective, see Barbara Fredrickson, *Love 2.0: How Our Supreme Emotion Affects Everything We Feel, Think, Do, and Become* (New York: Hudson Street Press, 2013).

32. Lyubomirsky, *How of Happiness*, p. 129.

33. John Gottman, *The Seven Principles for Making Marriage Work: A Practical Guide from the Country's Foremost Relationship Expert* (New York: Three Rivers Press, 1999).

CHAPTER 3 The Way of Prayer

1. N. M. Lambert, F. D. Fincham, T. F. Stillman, S. M. Graham, and S. R. H. Beach, "Motivating Change in Relationships: Can Prayer Increase Forgiveness?" *Psychological Science* 21 (2010): 126–32.

2. R. H. Bremner et al., "'Pray for Those Who Mistreat You': Effects of Prayer on Anger and Aggression," *Personality and Social Psychology Bulletin* 37, no. 6 (2011): 830.

3. Andrew Newberg, *How God Changes Your Brain: Breakthrough Findings from a Leading Neuroscientist* (New York: Ballantine, 2009), p. 174.

4. Jonathan Haidt, *The Happiness Hypothesis* (New York: Basic Books, 2006), p. 48.

5. Barbara Fredrickson, *Love 2.0: How Our Supreme Emotion Affects Everything We Feel, Think, Do, and Become* (New York: Hudson Street Press, 2013).

6. Robert Emmons, *Thanks! How the New Science of Gratitude Can Make You Happier* (New York: Houghton Mifflin, 2007), p. 42.

7. Christopher Peterson, *A Primer in Positive Psychology* (New York: Oxford University Press, 2006), p. 33.

8. Roy Baumeister and John Tierney, *Willpower: Rediscovering the Greatest Human Strength* (New York: Penguin, 2011); Kelly McGonigal, *The Willpower Instinct: How Self-Control Works, Why It Matters, and What You Can Do to Get More of It* (New York: Penguin Books, 2012).

9. Walter Mischel, *The Marshmallow Test: Mastering Self-Control* (New York: Little, Brown, 2014).

10. Fredrickson, *Love 2.0*, p. 12.

11. St. Ignatius of Loyola, *Spiritual Exercises*, Third Method of Prayer.

12. Kai Kaspar, "Washing One's Hands After Failure Enhances Optimism but Hampers Future Performance," *Social Psychological and Personality Science* 4, no. 1 (2013): 69–73.

13. Chen-Bo Zhong and Katie Liljenquist, "Washing Away Your Sins: Threatened Morality and Physical Cleansing," *Science* 313, no. 5792 (2006): 1451–52; Spike W. S. Lee and Norbert Schwarz, "Wiping the Slate Clean: Psychological Consequences of Physical Cleansing," *Current Directions in Psychological Science* 20, no. 5 (2011): 307–11.

14. Chen-Bo Zhong, Brendan Strejcek, and Niro Sivanathan, "A Clean Self Can Render Harsh Moral Judgment," *Journal of Experimental Social Psychology* 46, no. 5 (2010): 859–62.

15. Spike W. S. Lee and Norbert Schwarz, "Washing Away Postdecisional Dissonance," *Science* 328, no. 5979 (2010): 709.

16. Haidt, *Happiness Hypothesis*, p. 237.

17. R. B. van Baaren, R. W. Holland, K. Kawakami, and A. van Knippenberg, "Mimicry and Prosocial Behavior," *Psychological Science* 15, no. 1 (2004): 71–74; S. S. Wiltermuth and C. Heath, "Synchrony and Cooperation," *Psychological Science* 20, no. 1 (2009): 1–5; E. E. Cohen, R. Ejsmond-Frey, N. Knight, and R. I. Dunbar, "Rowers' High: Behavioural Synchrony Is Correlated with Elevated Pain Thresholds," *Biology Letters* 6, no. 1 (2010): 106–8; M. J. Hove and J. L. Risen, "It's All in the Timing: Interpersonal Synchrony Increases Affiliation," *Social Cognition* 27, no. 6 (2009): 949–61.

18. Scott Hahn, *First Comes Love: Finding Your Family in the Church and the Trinity* (New York: Image, 2006).

19. Haidt, *Happiness Hypothesis*, p. 79.

20. Pride in used in Scripture in these two different senses. A disordered pride is condemned throughout Scripture (Proverbs 8:13; Luke 1:51). On the other hand, a minority of biblical passages use pride as a positive term. Romans 11:13 reads: "I am talking to you Gentiles. Inasmuch as I am the apostle to the Gentiles, I take pride in my ministry." Second Corinthians 7:4 reads: "I have spoken to you with great frankness; I take great pride in you. I am greatly encouraged; in all our troubles my joy knows no bounds." On positive senses of pride in Scripture, see also Psalm 47:4; Amos 8:7; Galatians 6:4.

21. Jean-Paul Sartre, *Existentialism and Human Emotions* (New York: Citadel Press, 1985), p. 63.

22. St. Thomas Aquinas, *Summa theologiae* I-II, q. 34, a. 1.

23. Tal Ben-Shahar, *Choose the Life You Want: The Mindful Way to Happiness* (New York: The Experiment, LLC, 2012), p. 230.

24. Fredrickson, *Love 2.0*, p. 84.

25. McGonigal, *Willpower Instinct*, p. 204.

26. Christopher Peterson, *Pursuing the Good Life: 100 Reflections on Positive Psychology* (New York: Oxford University Press, 2013), p. 317.

27. William Irvine, *A Guide to the Good Life: The Ancient Art of Stoic Joy* (New York: Oxford University Press, 2009), p. 71.

28. *The Wit and Wisdom of* G. K. *Chesterton*, selected and introduced by Bevis Hillier (New York: Continuum, 2010), p. 243.

29. Haidt, *Happiness Hypothesis*, p. 140.

30. Susan Kuchinskas, *The Chemistry of Connection: How the Oxytocin Response Can Help You Find Trust, Intimacy, and Love* (Oakland, CA: New Harbinger Publications, 2009), p. 135.

CHAPTER 4 The Way of Gratitude

1. Cited in *Oxford Treasury of Sayings and Quotations*, ed. Susan Ratcliffe (Oxford: Oxford University Press, 2011), p. 196.

2. Robert A. Emmons, *Gratitude Works! A 21-Day Program for Creating Emotional Prosperity* (San Francisco: Jossey-Bass, 2013), p. 10.

3. Philip C. Watkins, *Gratitude and the Good Life: Towards a Psychology of Appreciation* (New York: Springer, 2014), p. 15.

4. F. S. Bridges, "Rates of Homicide and Suicide on Major National Holidays," *Psychological Reports* 94, no. 2 (2004): 723–24.

5. Emmons, *Gratitude Works!*, p. 5.

6. Ibid.

7. Ibid., p. 16.

8. Ibid.

9. Ibid.

10. Anne Elizabeth Moore, "Milton Friedman's Pencil," *The New Inquiry*, December 17, 2012, http://thenewinquiry.com/essays/milton-friedmans-pencil/.

11. Robert Emmons, *Thanks! How the New Science of Gratitude Can Make You Happier* (New York: Houghton Mifflin, 2007), pp. 135–36.

12. St. Thomas Aquinas, *Summa contra Gentiles* 1.88.

13. Ibid., 1.28.

14. Eleonore Stump, *Wandering in Darkness: Narrative and the Problem of Suffering* (Oxford: Oxford University Press, 2012).

15. Emmons, *Thanks!*, pp. 148–49.

16. Thanks to Dr. Aaron Kheriaty, who pointed this out and supplied the words.

17. Emmons, *Thanks!*, p. 150.

18. Paul Wong, "I'm Glad That I'm a Nobody: A Positive Psychology of Humility" (November 2003), http://www.meaning.ca/archives/presidents_columns/pres_col_nov_2003.htm.

19. Pelin Kesebir, "A Quiet Ego Quiets Death Anxiety: Humility as an Existential Anxiety Buffer," *Journal of Personality and Social Psychology* 106, no. 4 (2014): 611.

20. Ibid., p. 610.

21. Sonja Lyubomirsky, *The How of Happiness: A New Approach to Getting the Life You Want* (New York: Penguin Books, 2007), p. 13.

22. Daniel Kahneman, *Thinking, Fast and Slow* (New York: Farrar, Straus and Giroux, 2011), pp. 23–24.

23. *Spiritual Exercises of Ignatius Loyola*, with commentary by Joseph Tetlow (New York: Crossroad, 2009), pp. 67–68.

24. Emmons, *Thanks!*, p. 82.

25. Michael Craig Miller, "In Praise of Gratitude" (November 2011), http://www.health.harvard.edu/newsletters/Harvard_Mental_Health_Letter/2011/November/in-praise-of-gratitude.

26. Simon Schama, *A History of Britain*, vol. 3, *The Fate of Empire, 1776–2000* (New York: Hyperion, 2002), p. 537.

27. Emmons, *Gratitude Works!*, p. 30.

CHAPTER 5 The Way of Forgiveness

1. Christopher Peterson, *A Primer in Positive Psychology* (New York: Oxford University Press, 2006), p. 33.

2. Everett Worthington, *Forgiving and Reconciling: Bridges to Wholeness and Hope* (Downers Grove, IL: InterVarsity Press, 2003), p. 33.

3. Sonja Lyubomirsky, *The How of Happiness: A Scientific Approach to Getting the Life You Want* (New York: Penguin Books, 2007), p. 172.

4. Worthington, *Forgiving and Reconciling,* chap. 2.

5. Mark R. Leary and Sadie Leder, "The Nature of Hurt Feelings: Emotional Experience and Cognitive Appraisals," in *Feeling Hurt in Close Relationships,* ed. Anita L. Vangelisti (New York: Cambridge University Press, 2009), p. 17.

6. Joan O'C. Hammilton, "Peace Work," *Stanford Magazine,* May/June 2001, http://alumni.stanford.edu/get/page/magazine/article/?article_id=39032.

7. Viktor E. Frankl, *Man's Search for Meaning* (Boston: Beacon Press, 1984), p. 75.

8. Martin Seligman, *Flourish: A Visionary New Understanding of Happiness and Well-Being* (New York: Simon and Schuster, 2011), pp. 137–62.

9. Hammilton, "Peace Work."

10. Fred Luskin, *Forgive for Good* (New York: HarperCollins, 2002), p. 204.

11. Worthington, *Forgiving and Reconciling,* p. 18.

12. Martin Seligman, *Authentic Happiness: Using the New Positive Psychology to Realize Your Potential for Lasting Fulfillment* (New York: Simon & Schuster, 2002), p. 81.

13. Kelly McGonigal, *The Neuroscience of Change: A Compassion-Based Program for Personal Transformation*, Unabridged Audio CD (Louisville, CO: Sounds True, 2012).

14. Robert A. Emmons, *Gratitude Works! A 21-Day Program for Creating Emotional Prosperity* (San Francisco: Jossey-Bass, 2013), pp. 59, 60.

CHAPTER 6 The Way of Virtue

1. Sonja Lyubomirsky, *The How of Happiness: A Scientific Approach to Getting the Life You Want* (New York: Penguin Books, 2007), p. 275.

2. *Catechism of the Catholic Church* 1803, quoting Philippians 4:8.

3. St. Thomas Aquinas, *Summa contra Gentiles* 1.100–102.

4. For more on these topics, see Kristján Kristjánsson, *Virtues and Vices in Positive Psychology: A Philosophical Critique* (New York: Cambridge University Press, 2013).

5. St. Thomas Aquinas, *Summa theologiae* II-II, q. 23, a. 7.

6. Norman Doidge, *The Brain That Changes Itself: Stories of Personal Triumph from the Frontiers of Brain Science* (New York: Penguin Books, 2007).

7. Roy Baumeister and John Tierney, *Willpower: Rediscovering the Greatest Human Strength* (New York: Penguin Books, 2011), p. 114.

8. St. Ignatius of Loyola, *Spiritual Exercises*, [24–31], http://www.ccel.org/ccel/ignatius/exercises.xii.ii.html?highlight=examin#highlight. See also Timothy Gallagher, *The Discernment of Spirits: An Ignatian Guide for Everyday Living* (New York: Crossroad, 2005).

9. Baumeister and Tierney, *Willpower.*

10. Robert B. Cialdini, *Influence: The Psychology of Persuasion* (New York: Harper Business, 2006), p. 92.

11. Kelly McGonigal, *The Willpower Instinct: How Self-Control Works, Why It Matters, and What You Can Do to Get More of It* (New York: Penguin Books, 2012), chap. 9.

12. Charles Duhigg, *The Power of Habit: Why We Do What We Do in Life and Business* (New York: Random House, 2012).

13. St. Thomas Aquinas, *Summa theologiae* I-II, q. 7, a. 3.

14. D. W. Robertson, Jr., "A Note on the Classical Origin of 'Circumstances' in the Medieval Confessional," *Studies in Philology* 43, no. 1 (1946): 6–14.

15. Duhigg, *Power of Habit*, p. 143.

16. Jeremy Dean, *Making Habits, Breaking Habits: Why We Do Things, Why We Don't, and How to Make Any Change Stick* (Boston: Da Capo Press, 2013), p. 6.

CHAPTER 7 The Way of Willpower

1. Shawn Achor, *The Happiness Advantage: The Seven Principles of Positive Psychology That Fuel Success and Performance at Work* (New York: Crown Business, 2010), p. 146.

2. Edward St. Aubyn, *Mother's Milk* (New York: Open City Books, 2005), p. 106.

3. Second Vatican Council, *Gaudium et Spes* 62.

4. I am summarizing throughout this chapter many insights drawn from Kelly McGonigal.

5. Walter Mischel, *The Marshmallow Test: Mastering Self-Control* (New York: Little, Brown, 2014), pp. 7–8.

6. Roy Baumeister and John Tierney, *Willpower: Rediscovering the Greatest Human Strength* (New York: Penguin Books, 2011), p. 132; Jeremy Dean, *Making Habits, Breaking Habits: Why We Do Things, Why We Don't, and How to Make Any Change Stick* (Boston: Da Capo Press, 2013), p. 165.

7. Dean, *Making Habits, Breaking Habits*, p. 162.

8. Kelly McGonigal, *The Willpower Instinct: How Self-Control Works, Why It Matters, and What You Can Do To Get More of It* (New York: Penguin Books, 2012), p. 42.

9. Roy Baumeister and John Tierney, *Willpower: Rediscovering the Greatest Human Strength* (New York: Penguin Books, 2011), p. 156.

10. Ibid., p. 137.

11. Mischel, *Marshmallow Test*, pp. 7–8.

12. Aristotle, *Nicomachean Ethics* 1166a10–38.

13. St. Thomas Aquinas, *Summa theologiae* II-II, q. 24, a. 4.

14. Everett Worthington, *Moving Forward: Six Steps to Forgiving Yourself and Breaking Free from the Past* (Colorado Springs, CO: WaterBrook Press, 2013).

15. McGonigal, *Willpower Instinct*, p. 90.

16. Ibid.

17. Ibid., p. 104.

18. Ibid., p. 117.

19. Ibid., p. 160.

20. Daniel Kahneman, *Thinking, Fast and Slow* (New York: Farrar, Straus and Giroux, 2011), p. 105.

21. Ibid. p. 256.

22. McGonigal, *Willpower Instinct*, p. 209.

23. Kevin Majeres, http://purityispossible.com/.

24. McGonigal, *Willpower Instinct*, p. 215.

25. St. Ignatius of Loyola, *Spiritual Exercises*, rule 13.

26. Mischel, *Marshmallow Test*, p. 34.

27. Ibid., p. 265.

28. *Catechism of the Catholic Church* 1708–9.

29. Baumeister and Tierney, *Willpower,* p. 113.

30. Ibid., p. 180.

31. Oscar Wilde, *The Picture of Dorian Gray* (CreateSpace Independent Publishing Platform, 2014), p. 14.

32. McGonigal, *Willpower Instinct,* p. 235.

33. Judith L. Kovacs, ed., *1 Corinthians: Interpreted by Early Christian Medieval Commentators* (Grand Rapids, MI: Eerdmans, 2005), p. 168.

34. C. S. Lewis, *The Complete C. S. Lewis Signature Classics* (New York: HarperCollins, 2007), p. 242.

35. McGonigal, *Willpower Instinct.*

36. Fulton J. Sheen, *Preface to Religion* (New York: P. J. Kenedy, 1946), p. 126.

37. McGonigal, *Willpower Instinct,* pp. 147–48.

38. Pope Pius XII, "On Psychotherapy and Religion" (address, April 13, 1953), 37.

39. Aaron Kheriaty, with Fr. John Cihak, *The Catholic Guide to Depression: How the Saints, the Sacraments, and Psychiatry Can Help You Break Its Grip and Find Happiness Again* (Manchester, NH: Sophia Institute Press, 2012), pp. 163–66.

40. Mischel, *Marshmallow Test,* p. 35.

41. C. J. Bryan, G. M. Walton, Todd Rogers, and Carol S. Dweck, "Motivating Voter Turnout by Invoking the Self," *Proceedings of the National Academy of Sciences* 108, no. 31 (2011): 12653–56.

42. Chip Heath and Dan Heath, *Made to Stick: Why Some Ideas Survive and Others Die* (New York: Random House, 2008), pp. 195–99.

43. McGonigal, *Willpower Instinct,* pp. 198–99.

44. Noah Goldstein, Steven J. Martin, and Robert Cialdini, *Yes!: 50 Scientifically Proven Ways to Be Persuasive* (New York: Free Press, 2009), p. 22; emphasis in the original.

45. Justin Taylor, "How Many Americans Attend Church Each Week?," the gospelcoalition.org, March 1, 2007, http://www.thegospelcoalition.org/blogs/justintaylor/2007/03/01/how-many-americans-attend-church-each/.

46. http://mashable.com/2014/02/03/super-bowl-viewers-ratings/.

47. Frank Newport, "Easter Season Finds a Religious, Largely Christian Nation," www.gallup.com, March 21, 2008, http://www.gallup.com/poll/105544/easter-season-finds-religious-largely-christian-nation.aspx.

48. Michael Lipka, "5 Facts About Prayer," pewresearch.org, May 1, 2014, http://www.pewresearch.org/fact-tank/2014/05/01/5-facts-about-prayer/.

49. Stanley Milgram, "Behavioral Study of Obedience," *Journal of Abnormal and Social Psychology* 67 no. 4 (1963): 371–78.

50. *Catechism of the Catholic Church* 406.

CONCLUSION

1. Paul Vitz, *Psychology as Religion: The Cult of Self-Worship*, 2nd ed. (Grand Rapids, MI: Eerdmans, 1995).

2. Robert Kugelmann, *Psychology and Catholicism: Contested Boundaries* (New York: Cambridge University Press, 2011).

3. Friedrich Nietzsche, *The Antichrist* (New York: Soho Books, 2013) 56; *Jenseits von Gut und Böse* (Milton Keynes, UK: JiaHu Books, 2013) IV, 168.

4. Martin Seligman, *Authentic Happiness: Using the New Positive Psychology to Realize Your Potential for Lasting Fulfillment* (New York: Free Press, 2002), pp. 12, 255.

5. Jonathan Haidt, *The Happiness Hypothesis: Finding Modern Truth in Ancient Wisdom* (New York: Basic Books, 2006), p. 71.

6. Ed Diener and Robert Biswas-Diener, *Happiness: Unlocking the Mysteries of Psychological Wealth* (Malden, MA: Blackwell, 2008), p. 4.

7. For more on this topic, see Everett Worthington, *Coming to Peace with Psychology: What Christians Can Learn from Psychological Science* (Downers Grove, IL: InterVarsity Academic, 2010); Eric L. Johnson, ed., *Christianity and Psychology: Five Views* (Downers Grove, IL: InterVarsity Press, 2010); and Siang-Yang Tan, *Counseling and Psychotherapy: A Christian Perspective* (Grand Rapids, MI: Baker Academic, 2011).